Medical
Hypnosis Primer

Medical Hypnosis Primer

Clinical and Research Evidence

Arreed Franz Barabasz

Karen Olness

Robert Boland

Stephen Kahn

Editors

International
Society of Hypnosis

Society for Clinical
and Experimental
Hypnosis

Routledge
Taylor & Francis Group
New York · London

Routledge
Taylor & Francis Group
270 Madison Avenue
New York, NY 10016

Routledge
Taylor & Francis Group
27 Church Road
Hove, East Sussex BN3 2FA

Printed in the United States of America on acid-free paper
10 9 8 7 6 5 4 3 2 1

International Standard Book Number: 978-0-415-87178-5 (Paperback)

Library of Congress Cataloging-in-Publication Data

Medical hypnosis primer : clinical and research evidence / edited by
    Arreed Barabasz ... [et al.].
        p. ; cm.
    Includes bibliographical references and index.
    ISBN 978-0-415-87178-5 (pbk. : alk. paper)
    1. Hypnotism--Therapeutic use. I. Barabasz, Arreed F. II. Title.
    [DNLM: 1. Hypnosis--methods. 2. Evidence-Based Medicine--methods.
WM 415 E93 2009]

RC495.M435 2009
616.89'162--dc22
                                                    2009015850

Visit the Taylor & Francis Web site at
http://www.taylorandfrancis.com

and the Routledge Web site at
http://www.routledgementalhealth.com

Contents

Editors

Arreed Franz Barabasz, EdD, PhD, ABPP is a psychologist in practice and professor at Washington State University. He is past president of the Society for Clinical and Experimental Hypnosis and the American Psychological Association Div. 30. He is the editor of the *International Journal of Clinical and Experimental Hypnosis*, author of award-winning *Hypnotherapeutic Techniques, 2E*, published by Routledge, and the 2009 winner of the Distinguished Science Award in Hypnosis from the American Psychological Association. He conducts hypnosis training workshops worldwide.

Karen Olness, MD, FAAP, ABMH, is a professor of pediatrics, family medicine, and global health at Case Western Reserve University. She is past president of the American Society of Clinical Hypnosis, the Society for Clinical and Experimental Hypnosis, the International Society of Hypnosis, and the Society for Developmental and Behavioral Pediatrics. She is the author of award winning book *Hypnosis and Hypnotherapy with Children*. She conducts hypnosis training workshops worldwide.

Bob Boland, MD, MPH (Johns Hopkins), DBA, ITP (Harvard) is currently a professor at the International University in Geneva, Switzerland. He trained at Johns Hopkins in preventive medicine and international health, and worked with the International Labor Office in Geneva on research projects for the management of environmental issues in 30 countries.

Stephen Kahn, PhD, is a psychologist in practice. Currently, he is professor of psychology and director of the Clinical Hypnosis Program at Adler School of Professional Psychology. He is past president and fellow of the Society for Clinical and Experimental Hypnosis and is the author of two books and numerous articles on hypnosis. He is also director of the Institute for Clinical Hypnosis and Research in Chicago.

Contributors

Assen Alladin, PhD
Foothills Medical Centre
University of Calgary
Calgary, Alberta, Canada

Professor Arreed Barabasz, EdD, PhD, ABPP
Laboratory of Hypnosis Research
Washington State University
Pullman, Washington

Ciara Christensen, PhD Candidate
Laboratory of Hypnosis Research
Washington State University
Pullman, Washington

Professor Jacqueline M. Irland, MD, PhD
University of Wisconsin
Madison, Wisconsin

Professor Mark P. Jensen, PhD
Department of Rehabilitation Medicine
University of Washington
Seattle, Washington

Professor Stephen Kahn, PhD
Adler School of Professional Psychology
Chicago, Illinois

Professor Daniel P. Kohen, MD
Department of Pediatrics
Department Family Medicine and Community Health
University of Minnesota
Twin Cities, Minnesota

Associate Professor Elvira V. Lang, MD, FSIR, FSCEHJ
Interventional Radiology
Harvard Medical School
Boston, Massachusetts

Hypnalgesics, LLC
Brookline, Massachusetts
www.hypnalgesics.com

Professor Karen Olness, MD, FAAP, ABMH
Department of Pediatrics
Department of Family Medicine and International Health
Case Western Reserve University
Cleveland, Ohio

Professor David R. Patterson, PhD, ABPP, ABPH
Department of Rehabilitation Medicine
University of Washington
Seattle, Washington

Professor David Spiegel, MD, PhD
Department of Psychiatry & Behavioral Sciences
Stanford University School of Medicine
Stanford, California

Linda Thomson, PhD, MSN, APRN
University of Vermont
Burlington, Vermont

Professor Eric Vermetten, MD, PhD
Military Mental Health
University Medical Center
Utrecht University
Utrecht, The Netherlands

Michael Yapko, PhD
Fallbrook, California

Introduction

Hypnosis has been used as an adjunct to medical practice for a very long time. It is routinely taught in over one-third of accredited schools of medicine and in PhD and diploma programs in clinical and counseling psychology. Medical hypnosis is grounded in an enormous foundation of empirical work that substantiates its efficacy under a variety of circumstances. (For recent evidence-based reviews, see Barabasz & Watkins, 2005; special issues of the *International Journal of Clinical and Experimental Hypnosis* ["Irritable bowel syndrome," vol. 54(1), 2006, and "Evidence-based practice in clinical hypnosis—Parts I and II," vol. 55(1–2), 2007], and earlier reviews by Lynn, Kirsch, Barabasz, Cardena, & Patterson, 2000; Patterson & Jensen, 2003).

The National Institutes of Health technology assessment panel ("Integration," 1996) recognizes hypnosis in the treatment of a variety of disorders and recommends its integration into medical interventions. Similarly, the American Medical Association officially approved the teaching of hypnosis in 1958 for clinical purposes, as did the American Psychological Association in 1960. The major international hypnosis societies—the Society for Clinical and Experimental Hypnosis (SCEH) and the International Society of Hypnosis (ISH)—hold memberships in the American Association for the Advancement of Science and the World Federation for Mental Health.

Hypnosis is not just effective but superior to a number of standard treatment procedures. For example, Elvira Lang and her colleagues at Harvard Medical School (Lang et al., 2000) found hypnosis to have significantly more pronounced effects on pain and anxiety reduction for invasive medical procedures, in contrast to structured attention, intravenous analgesia, or empathy. Furthermore, the effects are not limited to adult populations. Hypnosis is superior to hospital and distraction protocols for ethnically diverse, severely ill children (cancer or blood disorders) undergoing painful medical procedures (Smith, Barabasz, & Barabasz, 1996). Hypnotizable children (the majority) showed significantly lowered pain, anxiety, and distress scores in response to hypnosis, in contrast to low hypnotizable children, and were superior to standard pain amelioration interventions. Hypnosis also required fewer hospital staff members and less procedural time.

Hypnosis is cost effective, especially for developing countries where the cost of standard medical therapies may be prohibitive. Those properly trained in hypnosis will have a unique advantage for their patients and practice units. For decades, researchers merely alluded to the cost effectiveness of hypnotic interventions.

A major Harvard Medical School study (Lang & Rosen, 2002) revealed findings that are astonishing to those unfamiliar with hypnosis. The average cost associated with standard sedation for a range of outpatient procedures was $638, compared with $300 for sedation with adjunctive hypnosis. The addition of hypnosis resulted in a savings of $338 per case. If hypnosis were provided to all patients having surgical lumpectomy, $772.71 could be saved per case (Montgomery et al., 2007).

One can only speculate about the cost effectiveness produced by the greater improvement. However, Kirsch, Montgomery, and Sapirstein's (1995) meta-analysis showed an average 70% greater long-term effect when hypnosis was added to cognitive-behavioral therapies. Similar to the Lang and Rosen (2002) findings, Barabasz and Barabasz (2000) demonstrated both significantly increased clinical effectiveness and a reduction in treatment time by nearly 50% when hypnosis was added to specific applied psychophysiological treatment interventions.

Hypnosis is particularly effective in the treatment of mental health, both acute and chronic disorders. Watkins and Watkins (1997, pp. 162–194) summarized the effectiveness of ego state therapy and hypnoanalysis. Both procedures were found to be superior to psychodynamic therapies in general, particularly for posttraumatic stress disorder (PTSD).

Recently, Watkins and Barabasz (2008; see also Watkins & Watkins, 1997, pp. 162–194) demonstrated that intensive ego state therapy is an effective brief therapy for seriously rooted mental disorders. Hypnosis-based therapy can, in as little as 12 hours, often

achieve permanent, structural personality changes, including resolution of chronic, deeply rooted disorders.

Those using cognitive-behavioral therapies will no doubt be
impressed by the comprehensive meta-analysis of hypnosis as
an adjunct (Kirsch et al., 1995). The analysis was performed on
18 studies in which cognitive-behavioral therapy was compared
with the same therapy supplemented by hypnosis. The results indicated that the addition of hypnosis substantially enhanced treatment outcome, so the average patient receiving cognitive-behavioral
hypnotherapy showed greater improvement than at least 70% of
the patients receiving the nonhypnotic treatment. These results are
striking because of the limited studies, which emphasize procedural
differences between the hypnotic and nonhypnotic treatments.

Unfortunately, however, despite the plethora of evidence favor-
ing the widespread use of hypnosis, there remains much ignorance
on the part of some physicians and psychologists concerning it.
A number of practitioners still confuse the effects of hypnosis with
those that can be wrought by suggestion/placebo; others misconstrue
its effects on pain relief as nothing more than the effects of relax-
ation/suggestion (Barabasz & Watkins, 2005; McGlashan, Evans,
& Orne, 1969). In the mental health sphere, some psychoanalysts
parrot objections to hypnotherapy based on unverified theoretical
positions voiced by Freud nearly a century ago. It is no wonder that
so few practitioners today are skilled in the use of hypnosis. The
bottleneck seems to be that skill in hypnotherapy is limited to a
few practitioners, in contrast to the many who have mastered traditional interventions for mental and physical disorders.

Due to the recognition of hypnosis by the American Association
for the Advancement of Science, the World Federation of Mental
Health, the Royal College of Physicians and Surgeons, the American
Medical Association, and the American Psychological Association
it seems clear that training in hypnosis should be more widely available. Even those limited to basic cognitive-behavioral treatments
will find a dramatic enhancement of long-term outcomes with the
addition of hypnosis (Kirsch et al., 1995).

For those interested in learning about hypnosis or who would
like to develop their skills further, participation in scientific conferences with workshops in hypnosis is recommended. The major
international scientific societies in the field (i.e., SCEH and ISH;
see Appendix C) offer workshops worldwide, up to about a week
in length, at their annual meetings and onsite in a wide range of

countries. Workshops conducted by physicians and psychologists from the majority of hypnosis societies are comprised of several training components. They commonly include brief lectures, demonstrations of hypnotic inductions for specific disorders, and discussions interspersed with practical experiences, which gradually introduce new students to various hypnotic phenomena and the techniques for eliciting them. Presentations range hierarchically from simple to more complex. Theories of hypnosis are simplified and directly related to the application of hypnosis to medical requirements.

Marianne Barabasz, EdD

Objectives

This brief book contains chapters by top hypnosis authorities. It is intended to

1. Briefly present the basic concepts of modern medical hypnosis.
2. Encourage health care practitioners to learn how to use hypnosis as an adjunct to standard medical care.
3. Support teaching and practice of hypnosis as a part of the required syllabus for every medical and nursing school as well as graduate programs in clinical and counseling psychology.

How to Use the Book

The book is a brief introduction to hypnosis; it is not a training manual. Teaching texts are available elsewhere (Barabasz & Watkins, 2005; Olness & Kohen, 1996, 3rd ed.; Spiegel & Spiegel, 2004; Watkins & Barabasz, 2008). Such manuals are intended to be used in the context of hypnosis training as offered by the recognized national and international hypnosis organizations listed in Appendix C. The book is supplemented by the DVD, *Hypnotic Induction Demonstrations: Techniques, Metaphors, and Scripts.* Available from www.arreedbarabasz.com, www.amazon.com, or e-mail direct from ijceh@pullman.com by A. Barabasz and C. Christensen, 2009.

Bob Bolland, MD

Chapter 1

Hypnosis concepts

Arreed Barabasz and Ciara Christensen

1.1 OVERVIEW

Hypnosis is a set of procedures used by health professionals to treat a range of physical and emotional problems. One can enter this altered state of awareness spontaneously. However, for health care purposes it is attained by an induction procedure appropriate to the patient and the disorder.

Most hypnotic inductions engage patients' imaginative capacities and include hypnotic suggestions for focused attention, relaxation, and calmness. Inductions used for medical or psychological emergencies or children may use eyes-open protocols (alert hypnosis) and often use hypnotic suggestions for alertness (Olness & Kohen, 1996).

Patients respond to hypnosis in different ways. Some describe their experiences as a state of deepened awareness, others as a calm state of focused attention. Patients usually enjoy the experience and view it as very pleasant. The practitioner serves as the therapeutic agent/facilitator to guide the patient to achieve this pleasant state with hypnotic suggestions to alter perception, thought, and action.

If the responses to hypnotic suggestions satisfy a criterion, it is inferred that the procedure produces a hypnotic state. "Hypnotic responses are those responses and experiences characteristic of the hypnotic state" (Killeen & Nash, 2003, p. 208; Nash, 2005). The best results are obtained in the context of a constructive inter-personal practitioner–patient relationship (Kahn & Fromm, 2001, p. xiv), but hypnosis can also be induced in less than a minute of time to meet emergency medical demands (Barabasz & Watkins, 2005, pp. 54, 131–132).

Most people in the general population respond to hypnosis. Those who respond well to hypnosis are usually not gullible; neither are

1

they more responsive to placebos, social pressures, or authority figures than those who do not respond well to hypnosis. The hypnotic state can be entered without a formal induction. This is a common response to a trauma-inducing event (Spiegel & Spiegel, 2004; Watkins & Barabasz, 2008; van der Kolk, 1994; van der Kolk, McFarlane, & Alexander, 1996; van der Kolk, Pelcovitz, et al., 1996).

1.2 COMMON EVIDENCE-BASED USES OF HYPNOSIS

The references following each common use of hypnosis cited in the following list summarize the most recent evidence-based and clinical efficacy data available in addition to the present brief volume. The majority of study abstracts are available online at no charge via the *International Journal of Clinical and Experimental Hypnosis (IJCEH)*, Web page (http://www.ijceh.com). There are many other legitimate uses of hypnosis supported by the scientific literature. The following list cites only the most common uses of the modality. To review the enormous number of studies and clinical data on hypnosis and psychotherapy is beyond the scope of this brief volume. Some of the most common evidence-based uses are

1. Acute and chronic pain, including medical procedures and pre- and postoperative surgeries (Elkins, Jensen, & Patterson, 2007; Flory, Martinez-Salazar, & Lang, 2007)
2. Posttraumatic stress disorder, PTSD (Lynn & Cardena, 2007; Watkins & Barabasz, 2008)
3. Childhood and adolescent problems (Olness & Kohen, 1996; this volume, chap. 5)
4. Childbirth pain and trauma (Barabasz & Watkins, 2005; Brown & Hammond, 2007; this volume, Chapter 8)
5. Insomnia (Graci & Hardie, 2007; Yapko, 2006)
6. Depression (Alladin & Alibhai, 2007; Yapko, 2006; also IJCEH Special Issue on Hypnosis for Depression, in press, early 2010)
7. Weight control/healthy eating/exercise (M. Barabasz, 2007; Kirsch, 1996)
8. Psychosomatic disorders (Flammer & Alladin, 2007)
9. Habit control (Barabasz & Watkins, 2005; Spiegel & Spiegel, 2004)

10. Irritable bowel syndrome, IBS (Irritable bowel syndrome, Paulson, 2006; Golden, 2007; IJCEH Special Issue on Hypnosis for IBS, 2010)
11. Headaches and migraines (Hammond, 2007)
12. Cancer patient care (Neron & Stephenson, 2007)
13. Human papillomavirus, HPV (currently under study as a possible treatment of choice versus standard medical care but not yet fully evidence based; Barabasz, Higley, Christensen, & Barabasz, 2009; Gruzelier et al., 2002).

1.3 HYPNOSIS DEFINED

A short definition of hypnosis is an "attentive perception and concentration, which leads to controlled imagination" (Spiegel, 1998, p. 2). The hypnotic experience might be best explained to new patients as being very much like the experience one may have when absorbed in a good book, a movie, or even watching cloud shapes change in the sky (Barabasz, 1984; Tellegen & Atkinson, 1974). Most published researchers recognize hypnosis as "primarily an identifiable state" (Christensen, 2005).

Hypnosis operates from one's latent cognitive ability (hypnotizability), which influences the extent of the responses. Contrary to common belief, social influences such as "expectancy" have only a modest influence on genuine hypnotic responsiveness (Barabasz & Perez, 2007; Benham, Woody, Wilson, & Nash, 2006).

The initial suggestion can constitute the hypnotic induction (Nash, 2005), but medical hypnotic inductions usually involve progressive phases of facilitation on the part of the health care practitioner. This is usually done to help the patient attain a state of hypnosis with a depth suitable for a medical or psychotherapeutic purpose.

The hypnotic state is characterized by the patient's ability to sustain a state of attention, receptive, and intense focal concentration with diminished peripheral awareness. The hypnotic state occurs in an alert patient who has the capacity for intense involvement with a single point in space and time. Thus, the hypnotic state involves a contraction of awareness of involvement with other points in space and time. The intense focal attention necessitates the patient's elimination of distracting or irrelevant stimuli, thereby creating dialectic between focal and peripheral awareness (Spiegel & Spiegel, 2004). The physiological hypnotic state can occur spontaneously (Barabasz, 2005–2006; Spiegel & Spiegel, 2004). However, for medical procedures, the hypnotic state is induced under the guidance of the practitioner. It is best understood as both an altered state of consciousness and an interpersonal relationship of trust. Relaxation effects, although not required, are often a by-product of hypnosis. Individuals with the ability to enter hypnosis attend only to a given task while simultaneously freeing themselves from distractions (Barabasz & Watkins, 2005).

1.4 HYPNOTIZABILITY

Hypnosis is not a "special process" with a one-dimensional electroencephalogram (EEG) brain signature where, when experiencing a hypnotic state, a light bulb of sorts flashes on the patient's forehead. Rather than a simple matter of "either–or," research shows that reliable physiological correlates reflect the various subjective states perceived by the patient, as shown by EEG, event-related potential (ERP), and positron emission tomography (PET; Barabasz, 2000, 2005–2006; Barabasz & Barabasz, 2008; Barabasz et al., 1999; Fingelkurts, Fingelkurts, Kallio, & Revonsuo, 2007; Killeen & Nash, 2003; Kosslyn, Thompson, Constantine-Ferrando, Alpert, & Spiegel, 2000; Spiegel & Spiegel, 2004).

Hypnosis is also a matter of degree. Some individuals may enter a deep state and exhibit behaviors such as regression, time distortion, and hallucinations, all of which can be elicited by various hypnotic inductions. Others, however, may reach a plateau, where they are able to experience only simple suggestions but not ones involving varying degrees of distortions of perception, such as might be required for surgical pain control.

There is a latent cognitive ability, best termed hypnotizability (Christensen, 2005) that strongly influences hypnotic responsiveness, which operates alongside the much more modest influence of situation and attitude (Benham et al., 2006).

The practitioner is concerned with the degree of "depth" to which a patient can be expected to respond. Some hypnotherapeutic techniques and experimental research responses require deep states (e.g., surgery). Others can be effectively employed with the patient only lightly hypnotized (e.g., minor medical procedures,

IBS [Barabasz & Barabasz, 2006], HPV [Barabasz et al., 2009], and many forms of psychotherapy).

Researchers and clinicians alike generally first assess the level of hypnotizability and then the level of depth capability. It is a common mistake to assume that because a patient has shown a high score on a reputable standardized scale of hypnotizability they are somehow automatically able to achieve adequate depth once hypnosis is induced. Such is not the case. It is no surprise to see that the scales of hypnotizability, useful as they are, only predict responses to hypnosis about 50% of the time (Hilgard, 1979).

Efforts should be made to assure adequate depth, which will vary throughout the period of hypnosis, depending on the receptivity of the patient to the induction and deepening procedures. Depth may also vary for dynamic reasons according to the demands placed upon the patient by specific suggestions. When depth is an issue, such as might be required to achieve a pain relief response during a medical procedure, it should be monitored by patient report (see Hilgard & Tart, 1966; McConkey, Wende, & Barnier, 1999).

Prior to using hypnosis, it is advisable to familiarize the patient with "hypnotic-like" experiences to reinforce debunking of myths about hypnosis and to ameliorate potential underlying fears about the modality. This will also help build rapport and trust. These brief informal clinical tests are very useful in evaluating patients for possible hypnotherapy. They not only serve to screen and evaluate, but their very administration can establish a positive psychological set and make later inductions of hypnosis easier (see Barabasz & Watkins, 2005, for protocols). (Standardized clinical testing of hypnotizability is explained in Chapter 2.)

1.5 LEARNING HOW TO USE HYPNOSIS FOR YOUR PATIENTS

Healthcare practitioners should take workshops taught by doctors of psychology (PhD, EdD, PsyD) or medicine (MD, MB ChB) who are known to be workshop leaders from the major hypnosis societies (such as the Society for Clinical and Experimental Hypnosis [SCEH], International Society of Hypnosis [ISH], and Milton H. Erickson Gesellschaft für Klinische Hypnose e.V. [MEG]). These workshops should be at least 20 to 24 hours and include hypnosis technique demonstrations, a minimum of 6 hours of supervised practice, and didactic information.

After taking basic training the professional should seek a mentor who, by phone or e-mail, can provide guidance and support. Workshop leaders who participate in worldwide outreaches and teach at hospital sites may be able to provide the initial on-site supervision with actual patients for a few days following the formal training. Fortunately, hypnosis is well accepted by most patients and this helps to reinforce new practitioners' confidence. Hypnotherapeutic technique skills should be reinforced by attending follow-up workshops and watching videos of other teachers. Reading and practice from the basic hypnotherapeutic techniques textbooks is of first importance. The top texts provide specific protocols for specific disorders (see Appendix D). Once read they will continue to serve as quick reference sources.

Practitioners can learn about the latest hypnosis research and clinical breakthroughs in the *IJCEH*. The *IJCEH* is the major journal in the field and is abstracted in more than 15 languages. Institutional subscriptions make the journal available to hospitals, universities, and clinics. These can be obtained online and in hard copy (contact: julie.ehlers@taylorandfrancis.com). Other professional hypnosis societies also produce journals.

Advanced training through workshops can lead to board certification. There are hypnosis board competency examinations in four areas: medicine, dentistry, psychology, and clinical social work.

1.6 EXAMPLE OF A HYPNOTIC-LIKE EXPERIENCE

The arm-drop test (adapted by the authors in abbreviated form from Barabasz & Watkins, 2005, pp. 94–99) serves as a prehypnotic experience that exemplifies the attention, concentration, and imaginative engagement that would be further facilitated by an actual hypnotic induction.

It is generally unwise to base an assessment of a person's ability to enter hypnosis on a single item (Barabasz, 1982). However, a clinically urgent situation may impose time constraints. In the opinion of Barabasz and Watkins (2005, p. 94), the arm-drop test is the single, most valuable test, in that it can be applied in a very short period of time.

The word *hypnosis* need not be mentioned to the patient. However, the arm-drop test provides an easily administered, rapid indicator of a patient's probable response to hypnotherapy. A positive response, indicated by both the patient's behavior and perception of the experience on this test, typically means that he or she is likely capable of responding favorably to a hypnotic induction. The practitioner is advantaged in that with a simple extension, the arm-drop test can be turned into an actual induction procedure if required by the clinical situation. Furthermore, the test permits the practitioner, especially one who is relatively inexperienced and not secure in his or her ability to induce hypnosis, to easily determine the patient's hypnotizability before committing to the use of hypnosis.

When practitioners are uncertain of their chances for success in inducing hypnosis with a certain patient, this lack of certainty is often initiated in the patient who becomes resistant to the induction procedure. This occurs not because the patient is unhypnotizable, but because the patient has perceived a lack of confidence in the practitioner.

When the arm-drop test is favorable, the practitioner, knowing that the patient is probably hypnotizable, begins his or her induction procedures with an air of confidence. This confidence then transmits to the patient and increases the likelihood of responsivity.

The patient is told, "I would like to test your reflexes. Would you please sit up straight in your chair or hospital bed (or stand) and extend both arms straight out in front of you, palms down." The patient then is asked to imagine, for example, a bucket, and that water is being poured into the bucket one liter at a time.

The following movements indicate hypnotizability:

1. The patient's perception of the experience is the key factor, outweighing the objective distance the arm drops.
2. The hand holding the bucket gradually lowers, showing either compliance or a veridical hypnotic response.
3. If the hand lowers somewhat, the inference is that the patient is responsive to hypnosis, but may be resistant, a slow responder, or capable of reaching only a light or medium trance. If the hand lowers rapidly, compliance rather than genuine hypnotic responding can be inferred.
4. The response that is most related to lack of hypnotizability is no response whatsoever.

Figure 1.1 The authors demonstrate an instant nonverbal induction for pain control (from Barabasz & Watkins, 2005).

One should never qualify or disqualify a patient for hypnosis on the basis of responses to a single test item, no matter how predictive it usually is. Patients respond to hypnosis on an individualized basis.

1.7 CONCLUSIONS

Hypnosis is an essentially culture-free treatment modality that has been shown to be effective in a wide range of medical and psychological disorders. It is an altered state of awareness involving attentive perception, concentration, and controlled imagination. For medical purposes, an induction procedure facilitated by the practitioner is employed. It is usually used adjunctively to facilitate standard care but can serve as a stand-alone procedure as required. Hypnosis is highly cost effective in contrast to standard medical care without hypnosis, well accepted by patients.

Figure 1.2 Rapid eye fixation induction.

Hypnosis may be the first-line treatment of choice but is most often used to complement standard medical and psychological interventions to improve patient tolerance (e.g., pain control with reduced medication), and initial and long-term treatment outcomes.

The ability for a patient to use hypnosis (hypnotizability) is a stable trait, easily measured by standardized procedures. Such measurement affords a fit between a specific procedure and patients'

Figure 1.3 Postural sway hypnotic-like experience.

responsiveness. The measurement procedure can lead directly to its use in the standard medical procedure.

The use of hypnosis significantly reduces treatment costs and increases patient satisfaction.

Chapter 2

Hypnosis testing

David Spiegel

2.1 INTRODUCTION

A huge variety of hypnotic induction techniques have been used over the past two centuries to elicit trance phenomena, ranging from eye fixation on fixed or moving targets, to eye closure, body sway, touch by the hypnotist, evoking numbness, paresthesias or paralysis, and so forth.

There is an important difference between the phenomenon of hypnosis itself and the ceremony that presumably elicits it. Trance phenomena may occur spontaneously or in response to a variety of induction ceremonies, as long as the patient has hypnotic capacity and is not aesthetically offended by the ceremony.

However, the premise of measurement is that variability in the hypnotic response has far more to do with the hypnotic capacity of the individual being hypnotized than the nature of the ceremony or the skill of the clinician inducing hypnosis. The hypnotic induction should be an occasion for both patient and therapist to discover the nature of the patient's hypnotic capacity, and work with the patient using that information. The hypnotic induction becomes a deduction.

This approach also eliminates artificial pressure on the practitioner and reduces anxiety on the part of the patient that something will be "done to" him or her, or that failure to enter the hypnotic state represents resistance. The clinical measurement of hypnotizability postulates that hypnosis is a subtle perceptual alteration involving a capacity for attentive, responsive concentration, which is inherent in the person and can be tapped by the examiner.

Clinical measurement of hypnotizability brings the use of hypnosis into the clinical arena as part of the medical and psychiatric/ psychological examination. The task of the clinician is to elicit and interpret information about the patient—nothing more, nothing less. In general, if the setting is appropriate for both the patient and the therapist, the transformation into trance occurs quickly and to the patient's optimal capacity. Repetition as a learning factor is usually of minor importance (Perry & Mullen, 1975). Although careful efforts to train higher hypnotizability do improve scores somewhat, preintervention hypnotizability accounts for most of the variance in final scores (Barabasz, 1982; Frischholz, Blumstein, & Spiegel, 1982). The trait outweighs attempted manipulation of the state.

2.2 MEASUREMENTS

What makes hypnosis a useful organizing concept in understanding its various ceremonies is the development of techniques for measuring a relatively stable trait—the capacity for hypnosis or hypnotizability. There are clinicians (Erickson, 1967) and researchers (T. X. Barber, 1969; Sarbin & Coe, 1972) who maintain that there are no reliable differences in hypnotic capacity. However, the preponderance of research in the last three decades, including my own, indicates that hypnotizability is a stable and measurable trait (Hilgard, 1965; Orne, 1959; Morgan, Johnson, & Hilgard, 1974; Perry & Mullen, 1975; Spiegel & Spiegel, 1978; Stern, Spiegel, & Nee, 1978).

This evidence has enabled research on hypnosis to flourish by allowing for comparison on a variety of dimensions between high and low hypnotizable individuals, and correlations between measured hypnotizability and a number of state and trait measures. Similarly, the measurement of hypnotizability in the clinical setting provides an opportunity for the clinician to use the phenomenon in a disciplined and knowledgeable manner.

Several well-standardized scales of hypnotizability, hypnotic capacity, and hypnotic susceptibility have been developed (Barber & Glass, 1962; Hilgard, 1965; Weitzenhoffer, 1980; Weitzenhoffer & Hilgard, 1962) with statistical reliability in mind. They were constructed as the summation score of a number of independent items, which on testing proved highly intercorrelated at a level of approximately 0.60 (Hilgard, 1965).

The Harvard Group Scales were designed so patients themselves could score themselves, allowing for group administration, but they correlate highly with scores obtained on the same patients using the Stanford Hypnotic Susceptibility Scale. These measures are lengthy to administer, requiring approximately 1 hour. From a clinical point of view there remained a need for an even shorter test of hypnotizability that would provide systematic information and at the same time facilitate the therapeutic atmosphere. The longer laboratory measures were not employed by busy clinicians and raised the additional problem of the development of fatigue during the testing.

Context and motivation are critical factors in any psychological measurement. Tests standardized with patients volunteering for the sole purpose of hypnotic experimentation measure different dimensions than those standardized on people presenting themselves for treatment (Frankel & Orne, 1976).

In the clinical context the assessment of hypnotizability is incidental to the treatment encounter and motivation is likely to be greater because the patient is seeking help with a personal problem rather than exercising curiosity. In this sense, paid volunteers for experimentation have a significantly different motivational set. Tests standardized on college student populations often reflect concern with only a limited sample of age and education, whereas the concern of the clinician must relate to the wide range characteristics of a patient population.

The traditional use of sleep terminology in earlier tests is misleading and can obscure the therapeutically useful mobilization of concentration, which characterizes trance. Some of the challenge items, such as hallucinating an insect, at times proved to be aesthetically disturbing to patients seeking relief from symptoms. Since hypnosis is an expression of integrated concentration, factors that impair concentration, such as drugs, psychopathology, and neurological deficits, should be taken into account.

2.3 CLINICAL TESTS OF HYPNOTIZABILITY

The Hypnotic Induction Profile (HIP; H. Spiegel, 1972, 1974; Spiegel & Spiegel, 2004) was designed for routine clinical use as well as research. A rapid procedure, the HIP takes 5 to 10 minutes to administer. It is both a procedure for trance induction and a disciplined measure of hypnotic capacity standardized on a patient population in a clinical setting. It is a measurement of hypnotizability in which a systematized sequence of instructions, responses, and observations are recorded with a uniform momentum in a standardized way, as the patient shifts into trance to the extent of his ability, maintains it, and then exits in a prescribed manner. Because the clinician standardizes his or her input, one can make the most out of variability in the patient's response.

Use of the HIP differs from traditional clinical induction techniques in that it is a measurement procedure and, in effect, the hypnotist is the measuring instrument. It differs from research scales of hypnotizability in being brief and clinically appropriate, as it has been more widely standardized on clinical populations.

Once a hypnotizability score is determined, the disciplined HIP procedure is no longer necessary. In general, subsequent inductions can be self-generated by the patient or signaled by the therapist. Indeed, the message to patients is that they can quickly learn to mobilize and use their own hypnotic capacity in the service of a variety of therapeutic goals. The time for the shift into trance is a matter of a few seconds.

The HIP is moderately and positively correlated with the Stanford Scales, with a range of correlations between .45 and .6, similar to the correlation of any one item of the Stanford Scale to the total score (Frischholz, Spiegel, Trentalange, & Spiegel, 1987; Orne et al., 1979; Sánchez-Armáss, Barabasz, & Barabasz, 2007). These significant correlations indicate that the scales are in the same domain but do not measure exactly the same thing. It is worth bearing in mind that any one item of the Stanford Hypnotic Susceptibility Scales correlates only about .6 with the overall score (Hilgard, 1965). Mean scores tend to be lower among the Stanford Scales and higher on the HIP.

2.4 OTHER CLINICAL SCALES

The need for brief clinical measures of hypnotizability that were practical and appropriate to the pressures of clinical work, and yet reliable and valid as a measure of the hypnotizability trait has been addressed in several other ways. The Hilgards introduced two scales: the Stanford Hypnotic Clinical Scale, which takes about 20 minutes (Morgan & Hilgard, 1975), and the Stanford Hypnotic

Arm Levitation Induction Test (Hilgard & Hilgard, 1975), which takes 5 minutes. Like the parent scales, these are additive measures with a series of ideomotor and challenge items.

2.5 STABILITY OF HYPNOTIZABILITY

There is strong evidence that hypnotizability is an extremely stable trait. Piccione, Hilgard, and Zimbardo (1989) tracked 50 former Stanford University undergraduates and blindly retested their hypnotizability on the Stanford Scales. The test–retest correlation over a 25-year interval was .71, which is higher reliability than one would observe in IQ over such a long interval. The finding means that one can predict half the variance in hypnotizability a quarter of a century later by knowing a patient's baseline hypnotizability score.

2.6 SETTING THE CONTEXT FOR TREATMENT

Many patients fear that hypnosis represents a loss of control. In fact, it is an opportunity to enhance their control over both mental and physical states. In hypnotizability testing there is an element of surprise that is also important. It is this very occasion that can be turned around to demonstrate to the patient how easily he can enhance and expand his own sense of control of himself and his body.

In discovering that utilizing intensely focused imagination can lead to an experience of less control or altered sensation in one arm and hand, for example, a patient learns to expand the limits of control. The clarification of this misconception about hypnosis can be employed to enhance a patient's own sense of mastery and to increase expectation of the opportunity for therapeutic change.

Hypnotizability testing can be used to decide whether it is worth attempting to employ hypnosis and, if so, how to use it. It is rare to have empirical information within 5 minutes that a treatment is not likely to work, leading to other choices, ranging from behavioral to biofeedback to psychopharmacological techniques. Furthermore, the degree of intact hypnotizability also serves as a useful clue to the style of interaction with the patient.

Highly hypnotizable individuals often want to know *what* to do, whereas low hypnotizables want to know *why*. The former want direction, the latter explanation (Spiegel & Spiegel, 2004).

Low hypnotizables often prefer various introspective, analytically oriented psychotherapies. Those who are mid-range in hypnotizability respond better to consolation and confrontation from the therapist. Highly hypnotizable individuals benefit most from firm guidelines to enhance their capacity to generate their own decisions and directions.

In summary, low hypnotizable patients do best with a therapeutic strategy that employs reason to free and mobilize affect; highly hypnotizable patients do best with a therapy that employs affective relatedness to the therapist in the service of enhancing rational control. Those in the mid-range respond to an approach that employs a balance of rational and affective factors in helping the patient confront and put in perspective his own tendency to oscillate between periods of activity and despair.

2.7 A METHOD OF SELF-HYPNOSIS

After you have completed the profile, you are in a position to teach the patient how he or she can utilize this capacity to shift into a state of attentive concentration in a disciplined way. This is how it is done:

> I am going to count to three. Follow this sequence again. One, look up toward your eyebrows, all the way up; two, close your eyelids, take a deep breath; three, exhale, let your eyes relax, and let your body float.
>
> As you feel yourself floating, you concentrate on the sensation of floating and at the same time you permit one hand or the other to feel like a buoyant balloon and allow it to float upward. As it does, your elbow bends and your forearm floats into an upright position. Sometimes you may get a feeling of magnetic pull on the back of your hand as it goes up. When your hand reaches this upright position, it becomes a signal for you to enter a state of meditation. As you concentrate, you may make it more vivid by imagining you are an astronaut in space or a ballet dancer.
>
> In this atmosphere of floating, you focus on this ... [Insert whatever strategy is relevant for the patient's goal, in a manner consistent with the trance level the patient is able to experience.

It is best to formulate the approach in a self-renewing manner that the patient is able to weave into his everyday lifestyle. The patient must sense that he can achieve mastery over the problem he is struggling with by "reprogramming himself"—often identified as an "exercise"—by means of a self-affirming, uncomplicated reformulation of the problem.]

Now, I propose that in the beginning you do these exercises as often as 10 times a day, preferably every 1 to 2 hours. At first the exercise takes about a minute; but as you become more expert at it, you can do it in much less time.

Reflect upon the implications of this and what it means to you in a private sense. Then bring yourself out of this state of concentration called self-hypnosis by counting backward this way: Three, get ready. Two, with your eyelids closed, roll up your eyes (and do it now). And, one, let your eyelids open slowly. Then, when your eyes are back in focus, slowly make a fist with the hand that is up and, as you open your fist slowly, your usual sensation and control returns. Let your hand float downward. That is the end of the exercise. But you will retain a general feeling of floating.

If necessary, demonstrate by doing it yourself. Then repeat the sequence of entering the trance state so that the patient can watch it. Then, while you supervise with direction, the patient repeats it again.

By doing the exercise every one to two hours, you can float into this state of buoyant repose. You have given yourself this island of time, 20 seconds every 1 to 2 hours, in which you use this extra receptivity to reimprint these critical points. Reflect upon them, then float back to your state of awareness, and get on with what you ordinarily do.

2.8 CONCLUSIONS

The systematic clinical assessment of hypnotizability can provide a great deal of information about a patient in a brief period of time. A person's capacity to use hypnosis, a stable and easily measurable trait, can provide a rational basis for choosing the type and style of psychotherapeutic treatment. This process also changes the nature of the initial interaction between therapist and patient, setting a context of empirical exploration rather than a battle of wills. From such clinical testing, both therapist and patient can learn about the patient's hypnotic capacity and the nature of hypnosis itself.

Chapter 3

Acute pain

David R. Patterson

3.1 OVERVIEW: USING HYPNOSIS FOR ACUTE PAIN

Acute pain is in most cases intense, shortly lived, and difficult to control. It usually arises from trauma, inflammation, or some sort of medical procedure; in other words, it is almost always linked to nociceptive input or tissue damage (Patterson & Sharar, 2001). A number of medical procedures can result in acute pain, including surgery, dentistry, burn wound debridement, chemotherapy, and labor and delivery.

One of the most time-honored applications of hypnosis is for the alleviation of acute pain. In the 1800s, Esdaile reported on the use of hypnosis as the sole anesthetic for hundreds of major surgeries (Hilgard & Hilgard, 1975). Over the past millennium, hypnosis has been reported in anecdotal reports to alleviate acute pain from about every type of etiology imaginable (Patterson & Jensen, 2003).

Pain control is possibly the area of medical hypnosis that has the most empirical support. For the past 20 years, we have seen a welcome increase on controlled studies that demonstrate that hypnosis is superior not only to control groups but to alternative interventions (Lang et al., 2000; Montgomery, DuHamel, & Redd, 2000; Patterson & Jensen, 2003; Patterson & Ptacek, 1997; Smith, Barabasz, & Barabasz, 1996). Not only does hypnosis often reduce patients' reports of pain and anxiety associated with procedures, it appears to show great promise in terms of cost offsets; this procedure can reduce medical costs associated with the use of costly anesthetics, the operating room, and the length of hospitalization (Lang & Rosen, 2002; Montgomery et al., 2007).

Acute pain is usually related to tissue damage or inflammation. As mentioned earlier, such tissue damage is often associated with medical care. Most surgery results in some form of trauma to the patient. Patients experiencing acute pain will frequently do so in one of two circumstances. First, they will often be undergoing some sort of medical crisis that might involve trauma (e.g., cuts, blunt force injury, amputations) or acute illness (e.g., sickle cell anemia, cancer). The second common cause of acute pain is from medical procedures. In many of these instances, the pain can be predicted, which gives the patient and clinician the ability to prepare for it. Such examples might involve dental work or childbirth.

Acute pain substantially interacts with psychological factors, particularly anxiety. Untreated pain of this nature is not only an excruciatingly unpleasant experience for the patient, it can often constitute threats to survival and the core well-being of those who experience it (Patterson, Tininenko, & Ptacek, 2006). As such, natural consequences of acute pain are fearfulness and anxiety.

Anxiety can have a cyclical interaction with acute pain and exacerbate its effects. With time, failure to address the anxiety associated with acute pain may make patients appear refractory to treatment (Patterson & Sharar, 1997). In other words, the conditioned anxiety from acute pain can become as significant a problem as the pain itself.

3.2 EVALUATING THE PATIENT WITH ACUTE PAIN

Evaluation of patients with acute pain is typically far less complex than for chronic pain. The interplay between acute pain and psychological factors is less difficult to tease apart than it is with chronic pain. At the same time, conducting a good assessment can facilitate our ability to address acute pain.

Acute pain that is not associated with a medical procedure is often a warning sign, and the first step of an evaluation is typically a thorough medical workup. It is assumed in this chapter that approaches to reduce acute pain are only pursued when it is clear that the pain is not signaling the need for acute medical intervention (e.g., appendectomy, removal of a tumor).

Medically, it is not only completely appropriate to treat patients aggressively with opioid analgesics as well as anesthetic agents, the failure to do so constitutes poor care (Melzack, 1990). Opioid analgesics (i.e., morphine and its derivatives) should be used in an anticipatory fashion. When used with a regular schedule to treat acute pain, such agents are seldom addicting. When addressing acute pain, patients should also be availed of a wide range of potential useful procedures such as epidural delivery of agents, patient controlled analgesia, blocks, and anesthetic agents.

It follows that medical evaluation of patients should include assessment of the patient's previous history of acute pain and trauma, as well as their potential response and side effects to interventions. Although often highly effective, medical interventions for acute pain do have a number of risks and complications (Brown, Albrecht, Pettit, McFadden, & Schermer, 2000; Cherny et al., 2001).

Psychological interventions for acute pain are usually warranted, not only because medical interventions can have side effects or risks, but also because some of them fail to address the entire problem. In most cases, psychological interventions are best used as adjuncts to medical ones. There is nothing about the use of opioid analgesics that precludes the use of hypnosis. However, the patient must be alert and attentive enough to attend to the induction; dose levels of medications that interfere with attention can reduce the effectiveness of hypnosis.

In terms of psychological assessment, clinicians should assess for a history of previous mental health disorders with particular attention to anxiety disorders. The interplay of anxiety with acute pain can frequently create the greatest complication. Patients with histories of problems with medical procedures may develop phobic reactions to future ones.

It is also useful to determine how patients tend to cope with medical procedures. Of particular note is whether they tend to be "repressors" or "sensitizers" in response to a medical procedure. In the former case, patients may cope better by avoiding the procedure as much as they can (Thompson, 1981). They do not wish for much information and would rather pretend that they are simply not present. Other patients may cope by gathering as much information as possible; such patients may also focus on the procedure with exquisite attention (Everett, Patterson, & Chen, 1990).

3.3 DEVELOPMENT AND NEGOTIATION OF THE TREATMENT PLAN

The patient in an acute pain crisis presents with treatment plan negotiation that typically differs dramatically from those with planned medical procedures. Once the medical reasons for an acute pain episode are determined, the goal of treatment becomes quite simply to reduce suffering as quickly as possible. Patients in acute pain crises are often in excruciating discomfort and may be terrified. Thorough histories are of minimal use in many cases and can detract from the time that should be spent in comforting the patient.

When working with patients that are anticipating a painful medical procedure, it is possible to take the time to establish a treatment plan. An interesting example is a treatment plan established by women undergoing childbirth. Since negotiating whether an epidural will be used is not always optimal when a patient is in labor, many choose to think through the pros and cons of such procedures well beforehand.

With procedural pain, clinicians can work with patients well in advance and apply information as well as cognitive-behavioral interventions over several treatment sessions to help the patient cope with a procedure long before it occurs. Presurgical evaluations are becoming increasingly commonplace and will not only address pain control, but will investigate factors that are likely to make the patient show better health outcome.

The clinician and patient should establish what the patient believes will be a successful outcome after a medical procedure. Reducing acute pain is only one aspect of this and many patients may have their attention on other health outcomes that could become part of the hypnotic treatment plan. Reducing recovery time and time back to work, improving sleep, and facilitating health-promoting behaviors are all examples of potential treatment plans well within the realm of hypnosis.

3.4 HYPNOSIS FOR ACUTE PAIN CRISES

The manner in which hypnosis is used will differ substantially based on whether the patient is in an acute pain crisis or is anticipating a medical procedure. Patients who are in acute pain at the time of intervention can present a great challenge for the use of hypnosis.

Hypnosis can be difficult because patients in acute pain may find it extremely difficult to focus their attention on this approach. At the same time, hypnotic techniques offer tools to the clinician that may be of substantial benefit if conventional medical or psychological approaches fail.

For patients who are in acute pain, presentation may be accompanied by anxiety, shallow breathing, and even some dissociation. When this is the case, the first component of an induction is to attempt to capture the patient's attention. If the clinician is successful in capturing attention, the patient may be brought to a surprisingly deep level of relaxation in a short amount of time (Patterson, 1996).

Relative to other applications of hypnosis, clinicians using this approach with acute pain crises may find themselves being much more direct and authoritarian with their suggestions than in less pressured situations. Induction strategies that allow the patient substantial choice or are slow and methodical will frequently be lost in this situation. Instead the clinician needs to recognize the patient's vulnerability and dependence, and take control in a respectful manner.

A typical patient in intense pain will show a surprising degree of trust and cooperation, and will proceed with an induction. If the patient is hesitant, more education about hypnosis might be warranted or the clinician should consider abandoning hypnosis altogether; it is simply wrong to believe that every patient is a candidate for hypnosis.

Once the patient has reached a level of relaxation, any number of suggestions can be made for comfort, relaxation, well-being, and rapid healing. Generally, finger signals are extremely useful for quick inductions.

3.5 HYPNOSIS FOR PROCEDURES THAT CAUSE ACUTE PAIN

Medical procedures can cause substantial pain and anxiety. However, relative to working with the patent in crisis as described earlier, the clinician has the luxury of being able to work with the patient before the procedure, hopefully several times, and ideally in calm, pain-free circumstances. A medical procedure will almost always be scheduled with some type of predictability and, even if that event only allows an hour of preparation, the clinician can still do a substantial amount of preparatory work with the patient. The steps for using hypnosis for anticipated procedures include the following:

1. Establishing rapport
2. Identifying stimuli associated with the upcoming procedure as well as a "safe place" for the patient
3. Performing the induction
4. Providing posthypnotic suggestions that are linked to cues associated with the procedure
5. Providing additional suggestions that might be of benefit

Before returning the patient to a waking state, the clinician can give the patient any number of additional posthypnotic suggestions based on his or her individual needs. These might include suggestions for improved sleep, healing time, or responses to other medical procedures.

3.6 CONCLUSIONS

Over the past 20 years, there has been a welcomed increase in controlled studies that demonstrate that hypnosis is superior not only to control groups but to alternative interventions (Patterson & Jensen, 2003). Pain control has become an area that has helped demonstrate the scientific legitimacy of clinical hypnosis. The majority of patients participating in hypnosis report some type of benefit (Montgomery et al., 2000). Not only does hypnosis often reduce patients' reports of pain and anxiety associated with procedures, it appears to show great promise in terms of cost offsets. Hypnosis can reduce medical costs associated with the use of costly anesthetics, the operating room, and the length of hospitalization (Lang & Rosen, 2002; Montgomery et al., 2007).

Chapter 4

Chronic pain

Mark P. Jensen

4.1 OVERVIEW

Chronic pain may be defined as pain that persists beyond the normal healing time after an injury, or as pain that is the result of an ongoing disease process (such as cancer or arthritis). Hypnotic interventions have been used to help individuals better manage chronic pain for many years, and there are hundreds of case reports illustrating hypnotic techniques that can benefit individuals with chronic pain (Patterson & Jensen, 2003).

It is only during the recent decades that controlled studies have demonstrated what clinicians have known all along: training patients with chronic pain to use self-hypnosis strategies can (a) reduce background daily pain, and (b) provide patients with specific skills they can use to reduce the severity and impact of pain when needed (Barabasz & Barabasz, 1989; Jensen & Patterson, 2006; Jensen & Patterson, 2006, 2008).

Any clinician working with an individual with chronic pain must keep in mind that chronic pain can be the result of, and be influenced by, many interrelated factors, including

1. Ongoing physical damage and resulting nociceptive input from nerves that transmit pain information to the central nervous system (which is responsible for nociceptive or non-neuropathic pain)
2. Previously damaged peripheral (outside the spinal cord) or central (within the brain or spinal cord) nervous system neurons (which are responsible for neuropathic pain)
3. Inactivity that results in weakened muscles and tendons, which then makes the patients more susceptible to injury
4. Discomfort from even normal activity

5. Overuse of muscles, tendons, and/or joints (e.g., repetitive stress injury)
6. Learning history (that is, the presence of a history of re-inforcement for pain and illness behavior); mood and distress; beliefs about the meaning of pain; and coping strategies (maladaptive strategies, such as pain-contingent rest or guarding) used to manage pain

All of these factors can be targeted for treatment, including hypnosis treatment. In fact, focusing on just one causal factor (or even on just one treatment modality) can limit the benefits that patients get from treatment.

Chronic pain often has a significant negative impact on many aspects of a patient's life. It can interfere with activities that the patient used to enjoy, interfere with sleep, contribute to marital or relationship discord, disrupt a patient's ability to work, and, in part because of these many other negative effects, cause or contribute to depression. A very large proportion of people with chronic pain meet criteria for a major depressive disorder (most studies report ranges between 30% and 54%; Banks & Kerns, 1996), and many more than this suffer from a number of depressive symptoms (Romano & Turner, 1985). Thus, assessing depression and treating it are important components of any adequate pain treatment plan.

Analgesic medications and rest are helpful to patients with acute pain problems (for example, just after major surgery). However, opioids and sedatives can contribute to greater disability in persons with chronic pain, and should therefore be avoided whenever possible (Fields, 2007; Fordyce, 1976).

On the other hand, self-hypnosis training has been demonstrated to benefit many patients with chronic pain (Jensen & Patterson, 2006; Montgomery, DuHamel, & Redd, 2000; Patterson & Jensen, 2003). Those benefits include reductions in the experience of pain, but also include many "side effects" such as improved sleep, increased ability to function despite pain, and improved mood and well-being.

4.2 EVALUATION OF THE PATIENT WITH CHRONIC PAIN

It is not appropriate to begin treatment for chronic pain until the patient has had a thorough medical and psychological evaluation.

The medical evaluation is needed to rule out any biomedical problems that would be responsive to appropriate medical interventions. For example, some neuropathic pain conditions respond positively to some anticonvulsants (gabapentin or pregabolin), and patients diagnosed with neuropathic pain who might respond to such treatments should be offered them. Perhaps even more important, a medical evaluation is critical for identifying and addressing any possible life-threatening illnesses that might be underlying the pain problem.

The medical evaluation should also yield specific recommendations regarding the extent to which changes in medication regimens may be needed, such as when the evaluating physician determines that opioids or benzodiazepines need to be tapered. Similarly, the medical evaluation can help determine the extent to which inactivity and guarding may be contributing to weakened muscles and tendons, which can both contribute to ongoing chronic pain. In this situation, appropriate physical therapy or graded reactivation programs are indicated. The clinician using hypnosis with the patient can incorporate hypnotic suggestions that would help the patient manage these recommended changes that result from the medical evaluation.

A thorough psychological evaluation is necessary to identify the psychological factors that may be contributing to the pain problem. For example, pain behaviors may play an important role in the management of a marital relationship. Patients with chronic pain may be so "pain focused" that they are unable to focus on any other aspect of their lives. They may report a pattern of exaggerated negative thinking about pain (catastrophizing), which has been repeatedly shown to be linked with poor outcomes (Boothby, Thorn, Stroud, & Jensen, 1999).

They may also report poor sleep hygiene and a lack of skills in being able to fall asleep. As mentioned earlier, significant depression and anxiety are also very common in people with chronic pain, and the contribution of these to the patient's suffering needs to be evaluated.

Finally, a belief that pain necessarily means that damage is occurring can contribute to a fear of movement (when movement results in increases in pain) and a lack of activity and participation in a regular exercise program (Vlaeyen & Linton, 2000). A clinician who proceeds with treatment with a goal of decreasing pain or pain behavior and who is unaware of the importance of the many psychological factors that could be contributing to these, will be less able to help the patient then a clinician who understands these factors and develops a treatment plan taking them all into account.

Certainly treatment plans that address only the patient's pain experience (for example, hypnosis treatment that only includes suggestions for decreased pain or what Barabasz and Watkins [2005] refer to as the suffering component of pain) and do not address other factors are very limited in scope (Patterson & Jensen, 2003). Instead, hypnosis and self-hypnosis training can and should be used to help address all of these other contributing factors, and also enhance the efficacy of other treatments that address these factors.

In short, an initial evaluation of the person with pain that includes an evaluation of the medical and psychological factors contributing to the pain problem, and the development of treatment goals that address all of these factors, is an essential first step of any treatment.

4.3 DEVELOPMENT AND NEGOTIATION OF THE TREATMENT PLAN

As a result of the medical and psychological evaluations, treatment goals will be identified. These goals can be more easily achieved if hypnotic interventions are utilized. These may include goals such as

1. Increased activity, mobility, and strength
2. Decreased use of analgesics or sedatives deemed inappropriate by the evaluation physician
3. Decreased overall (baseline) pain and increased ability to reduce pain using self-hypnosis skills
4. Improved sleep
5. Decreased anxiety/depression and increased well-being
6. Decreased pain focus (increased ability to ignore pain)
7. Decreased catastrophizing and other components of a negative cognitive set

There are a number treatments that have been shown to be effective for addressing all of these goals. These include graded activity and quota-based exercise programs (Vlaeyen, de Jong, Geilen, Heuts, & van Breukelen, 2002), nonpain contingent medication tapers

(Fordyce, 1976), sleep hygiene education (especially when combined with cognitive-behavioral therapy; Edinger, Wohlgemuth, Krystal, & Rice, 2005), cognitive restructuring (Turk, 2002), contingency management (Fordyce, 1976), and self-hypnosis training (J. Barber, 1996; Jensen & Patterson, 2006).

In fact, self-hypnosis training can be used to enhance the efficacy of many established pain treatments, and may be used directly to address the treatment goals of pain reduction, decreased pain focus, and improved sleep.

The reader interested in enhancing his or her clinical skills in chronic pain management is urged to become familiar with these interventions by

1. Attending conferences and workshops on these topics. Such workshops are often presented at meetings of the International Association for the Study of Pain (IASP), Society for Clinical and Experimental Hypnosis (SCEH), and International Society of Hypnosis (ISH). (See Appendix C for a list of hypnosis societies.)
2. Obtaining supervision from a clinician experienced with these interventions.
3. Reading the literature on the application of various treatments for chronic pain management.

4.4 HYPNOSIS FOR CHRONIC PAIN MANAGEMENT: INDUCTIONS

Whatever induction the clinician uses to initiate hypnosis with a patient, it can be helpful to ensure that each one begins with the same cue. Then, at the end of the session when any posthypnosis suggestions are made, one of these suggestions can include a specific link between the cue and subsequent hypnosis. By consistently using the same cue with a patient during training, that cue then gets linked to subsequent hypnosis, making it easier for the patient to use hypnosis on his or her own outside of the session by beginning self-hypnosis with the cue.

Although any one of a number of inductions can be used when using hypnosis with patients with chronic pain, it is practical to start with a relaxation induction (that is, a series of suggestions that the patient will experience each body part or muscle group as becoming increasingly relaxed and comfortable) for a number of reasons:

1. The great majority of individuals respond positively to a relaxation induction. Most people are able to experience changes in their subjective experience of relaxation, so the use of this induction contributes to positive outcome expectancies and self-efficacy.
2. A state of perceived relaxation is inconsistent with a state of suffering, so the induction itself can contribute to increased comfort.
3. The induction is one that is easy for patients to learn. After one or two experiences with it in the clinician's office, most patients are able to apply the induction at home when they want to practice self-hypnosis.

However, it is also a good idea to experiment with a number of inductions as treatment progresses, as patients differ in their responses to different inductions, and the best way to find what works best with any particular patient is to try several.

4.5 HYPNOSIS FOR CHRONIC PAIN MANAGEMENT: SUGGESTIONS TO ENHANCE OUTCOME

As emphasized throughout this chapter, clinicians rarely, if ever, should consider applying self-hypnosis training in people with chronic pain for only, or even necessarily primarily, the purpose of helping them experience a decrease in perceived pain. Most chronic pain treatment plans will have multiple goals, such as improved sleep, increased activity, tapering and eventual discontinuation of inappropriate analgesic or sedative medication use, participation in physical therapy, and decreased catastrophizing.

Many patients will also express some individual goals that they may have (help with anxiety management, increased confidence, a general sense of well-being) that are also responsive to self-hypnosis training. The patient may be participating in specific interventions or treatments to address these goals. Hypnosis can, and in many circumstances should, be used to facilitate and enhance the efficacy of other treatments that are being used to address these goals (Kirsch, Montgomery, & Sapirstein, 1995).

The suggestions that are appropriate for addressing these other factors would flow directly from the goals and the patient's stated difficulties with achieving them. In general, the suggestions would be designed to build confidence (self-efficacy), a perceived ability to achieve with relative ease (effortlessness), while experiencing at the least a neutral, but ideally a positive mood (perhaps a sense of distance or neutrality if this works for the patient, but the clinician may consider suggesting feelings of relaxation or even excitement). (See Barabasz & Watkins, 2005, for protocols.)

4.6 HYPNOSIS FOR CHRONIC PAIN MANAGEMENT: SUGGESTIONS FOR ANALGESIA AND COMFORT

When suggestions for analgesia and comfort are appropriate, it is helpful to remember that there are two (nonmutually exclusive) types of outcomes for hypnotic treatment of chronic pain:

1. A substantial and relatively permanent reduction in daily baseline pain
2. An increase in the patient's ability to reduce or ignore pain for a period of time (usually lasting for a number of hours but sometimes for days or longer; Jensen et al., 2008)

To the extent that both outcomes are desirable (and they almost always are), then suggestions for both are worth including in the treatment sessions.

Wording for suggestions for substantial and permanent changes in pain experience can be placed toward the end of the hypnosis session, when posthypnotic suggestions are usually given. Before this, the session would include whatever suggestions are deemed appropriate for the particular patient to help reduce or eliminate pain. Posthypnotic suggestions can be given to further these outcomes.

It is also wise to include wording to encourage and enhance patients' ability to use hypnosis to obtain relief and comfort whenever they choose. The majority of patients who learn self-hypnosis skills for pain management can learn to use hypnosis as a way to increase comfort when they wish during the day (in response to a cue for self-hypnosis). That is, they can learn to use an induction and subsequent self-suggestions to increase their experience of comfort, and the changes they are able to make often last for hours at a time.

4.7 CONCLUSIONS

It is important to remember that each patient responds to different hypnotic suggestions in unique ways (Barabasz & Watkins, 2005). So it is often wise to provide a wide variety of possible suggestions that the patient might benefit from at first, and gradually eliminate those the patient does not like or seem to respond to. The many categories of suggestions to try are limited only by the clinician's (and patient's; more often than not, the best ideas for suggestions are from the patient) imagination. Types of suggestions to consider include those that

1. Reduce the pain experience directly
2. Reduce the affective component of pain (how much any pain bothers the patient)
3. Increase the patient's ability to ignore pain
4. Alter the meaning of pain from a signal of harm or danger to a signal that has little meaning
5. Shift pain from a location that is more bothersome (e.g., low back) to an area that is less bothersome (e.g., the little finger)
6. Alter the quality of the sensation from one of "pain" to one of "pressure" or other not unpleasant sensation
7. Alter the patient's sense of time around any flare-ups (that they are perceived as lasting for very short periods of time)

Experienced clinicians differ in their use of audio recordings of sessions. Some insist that providing patients with such recordings increases dependence and limits the ability of patients to learn to use hypnosis on their own. Others argue that such tapes provide even more opportunities for patients to practice and thereby facilitate skill building. Preliminary research suggests that the availability of recordings may enhance outcomes, at least for some patients (summarized in Jensen et al., 2005). One approach would be to provide patients with audio recordings (as audio tapes or CDs) of the sessions, and invite them to listen to the tapes regularly and also to practice self-hypnosis without the tapes. They can then use whichever works best for them. Because the recordings can include posthypnotic suggestions for how to practice without the recordings ("Whenever you want to feel this good ... all you ever have to do is..."), use of the recordings can, in fact, reinforce a patient's ability to use hypnosis without the recording.

Chapter 5

Childhood problems

Karen Olness and Daniel P. Kohen

5.1 OVERVIEW

This chapter will provide information about areas in which hypnosis can help children, developmental considerations in working with children, hypnosis research with children, examples of helping children in pain with hypnosis, and guidelines for studying how to teach children self-hypnosis.

Children learn self-hypnosis easily. Normal children often play imaginary games; this talent can be adapted to help them develop skills in self-hypnosis. In fact, children naturally go in and out of hypnotic states as they become absorbed in pretend games, in reading a story, playing a videogame, or listening to music. The ability to use self-hypnosis provides children with a sense of personal participation in treatment and enhances their sense of mastery and competency.

Children may learn hypnosis as either primary or adjunct therapy for a variety of problems including

Habit problems such as nail biting, hair pulling, or thumb sucking (Olness & Kohen, 1996)

Chronic conditions, including migraine, asthma, hemophilia, diabetes, Tourette's, or cancer (Kohen & Zajac, 2007; Olness & Kohen, 1996; Olness, MacDonald, & Uden, 1987)

Performance anxiety including sports, music, speaking in front of the class, or test performance (Olness & Kohen, 1996)

Enuresis (Olness & Kohen, 1996)

Warts (Felt, Hall, Olness, & Kohen, 1998)

Conditioned fears or anxiety (Olness & Kohen, 1996)

Sleep problems: falling asleep, night-waking, nightmares, night terrors (Olness & Kohen, 1996)

Pain associated with procedures such as dental work, lumbar punctures, or venipunctures (Evans, Tsao, & Zeltzer, 2008; Kuttner, 1986, 1999; Smith, Barabasz, & Barabasz, 1996)
Chronic pain (Olness & Kohen, 1996)
Attention deficit disorders (ADD, ADHD; Anderson, Barabasz, Barabasz, & Warner, 2000; Barabasz, 2001; Barabasz & Barabasz, 2000; Warner, Barabasz, & Barabasz, 2000)

All of the above may be considered within the domain of evidence-based medicine.

Children reduce anxiety associated with pain by practicing self-hypnosis, and many children can also reduce the sensory component of pain. The teaching and application of self-hypnosis may be enhanced by providing a biofeedback opportunity to the child. This provides evidence to the child that changes in thinking result in changes in body responses.

5.2 PREPARING TO TEACH CHILDREN SELF-HYPNOSIS

Once the basic hypnosis workshop has been completed, practitioners who wish to teach self-hypnosis to children should take specialty workshops taught by health professionals who are experienced in working with children. These workshops should be at least 20–24 hours and include at least 6 hours of supervised practice of hypnosis techniques as well as didactic information.

After taking such basic training the professional should seek a mentor who, by phone or e-mail, can provide guidance and support. Fortunately, most children learn easily and benefit from the experience, and this is encouraging to the novice clinician-teacher.

The professional who is developing skills in teaching self-hypnosis to children should also attend follow-up workshops, watch video-tapes of other teachers, and read basic textbooks and hypnosis journals sponsored by professional hypnosis societies. There are hypnosis board examinations (of competency) in four areas: medicine, dentistry, psychology, and social work.

The professional who is developing skills in teaching self-hypnosis to children should learn and benefit from practicing self-hypnosis himself. Learning self-hypnosis is a valuable lifelong skill that provides many benefits.

5.3 RESEARCH IN HYPNOSIS WITH CHILDREN

Substantial research in child hypnosis has been done over the past 45 years. Initial research studied measures of child hypnotizability scales such as the Stanford Children's Hypnotic Susceptibility Scale. Most subsequent research has been clinical research that documents the efficacy of hypnosis with children in areas such as pain management, habit problems, wart reduction, and performance anxiety.

The variability in preferences, learning styles, and developmental stages among children complicates the design of research protocols that study hypnosis with children. These protocols are often written to describe identical hypnotic inductions, often tape-recorded, to be used at prescribed times. Measured variables do not include whether a child likes the induction, listens to the tape, or whether he or she focuses on entirely different mental imagery of his or her choosing. Furthermore, learning disabilities are often subtle and may not be recognized without detailed testing. Learning disabilities, such as auditory processing handicaps, may interfere with the ability of children to learn and remember self-hypnosis training. Each of these variables complicates efforts to perform meta-analyses on hypnosis and related interventions.

Interventions called relaxation imagery, imagery, visual imagery, or progressive relaxation each lead to a hypnotic state. Analyses of studies on efficacy of hypnosis in children should include all of these various strategies, which result in the induction of hypnosis in children.

Some research studies are defined as controlled but mix therapeutic interventions. For example, in Scharff, Marcus, and Masek's (2002) study titled "A Controlled Study of Minimal-Contact Thermal Biofeedback Treatment in Children with Migraine," children were randomly assigned to thermal biofeedback, attention, or wait-list control groups. The handwarming biofeedback group received four sessions of cognitive-behavioral stress management training, thermal biofeedback, progressive muscle relaxation, imagery training of warm places, and deep breathing techniques. Thus, these children were clearly also being taught self-hypnosis without calling it such.

Several controlled laboratory studies have demonstrated that there is an association between learning self-hypnosis and changes in humoral and cellular immunity in children. This work was the basis for research by Hewson-Bower and Drummond (1996, 2001) who demonstrated that training in self-hypnosis for children with frequent upper respiratory infections (URIs) resulted in a reduction of infectious episodes and fewer illness days if URIs did occur.

The International Society of Hypnosis (ISH) and the Society for Clinical and Experimental Hypnosis (SCEH; see Appendix C) are currently sponsoring Cochrane reviews of hypnotherapeutic interventions, including those with children.

5.4 ASSESSMENT OF THE CHILD

The child health professional who teaches self-hypnosis to children must, first, be knowledgeable and competent with respect to the presenting problem. For example, if a child has the presenting problem of enuresis, has a careful evaluation ruled out causes, such as a urinary tract infection, that would not respond to self-hypnosis? A dentist should not teach self-hypnosis to a child for enuresis, nor should a pediatrician do dental work.

It is important to know the child well before teaching him or her self-hypnosis. Is the problem more significant to parents or caretakers than to the child? Is the child motivated and interested in learning how he or she can help him- or herself? What are the child's likes, interests, dislikes, and fears? How does the child learn best? Formal assessment using the Stanford Clinical Scale for Children can be helpful (Morgan & Hilgard, 1979). Does the child have learning disabilities? What is the preferred mental imagery of a child? This may be visual, auditory, kinesthetic, and olfactory/taste. The teacher must consider all of these individual differences in developing a plan for teaching self-hypnosis with any given child.

5.5 APPROACHES TO TEACHING CHILDREN

It is essential that the coach or teacher emphasize that the child is in control and can decide when and where to use self-hypnosis. It is important to tell the child that self-hypnosis belongs to the child, that he or she needs to practice to become more skilled just as one must practice to learn soccer or some other sport; however, no one can force the child to practice.

Parents should be counseled to understand that self-hypnosis is a skill to be developed and refined and that only the child can do so, hopefully with their support and encouragement. They must be educated, however, to not remind the child to practice, although they may, in the beginning, discuss what type of reminder might be helpful to their child.

The choice of strategies for teaching self-hypnosis varies depending on the child's age and developmental stage. As children mature, their cognitive abilities change. Preschool children are very concrete in their thinking and, for this reason, the therapist must choose words very carefully. Children between ages 2 and 5 spend a great deal of their time in various types of behavior based on imagination and fantasy. They enjoy stories and may enter a hypnotic state as the parent or teacher reads a story to them. Unlike adults, they often prefer to do self-hypnosis practice with their eyes open.

Although adolescents may enjoy learning self-hypnosis methods that are similar to those preferred by adults, immature adolescents may prefer to use methods that also appeal to younger children. Children with cognitive impairment can learn self-hypnosis if the therapist selects a teaching approach appropriate for their actual developmental stage.

Because of developmental changes, an 8-year-old child is unlikely to enjoy a method he was taught at age 4. Therapists who work with children must be familiar with a variety of hypnosis induction strategies and be capable of creative modification to accommodate the changing developmental circumstances of a child.

5.6 SELF-HYPNOSIS AND PAIN MANAGEMENT

Based upon empirical work, training in self-hypnosis is very helpful in pain management for children (Olness & Kohen, 1996). Practicing self-hypnosis reduces the anxiety components of pain and also, as documented in recent studies, may reduce the sensory components of pain. Training in self-hypnosis is of special benefit to children with chronic pain illnesses such as sickle cell disease, hemophilia, cancer, or migraine. General principles for teaching hypnotic pain control include the following:

1. Assess one's personal experience about pain. The clinician who had negative experiences with painful procedures when he was a child may unconsciously project his fears and negative expectations onto his patient.

2. Assess parental perceptions and expectations about pain. Children are sensitive to their parents' fears and anxieties. It may be beneficial for parents also to learn self-hypnosis.
3. Consider the impact of the pediatric treatment team. The attitudes and expectations of adults on the treatment team are also understood by the child. Changes in the voice, movement, or demeanor of adults may increase anxiety in a child even before a procedure begins.
4. Consider the age and development of the child. For a toddler, a distraction approach, such as blowing bubbles, may be most appropriate.
5. Consider a child's interests, likes, and dislikes. It is easier to learn self-hypnosis if one can focus on something one enjoys.
6. Emphasize the child's control and mastery.
7. Select a pain assessment tool appropriate to the child and understood by the child. This might be a ruler if the child understands numbers. "Number 10 is a lot of discomfort and number 1 is a tiny bit of discomfort, and 0, of course, is no discomfort."
8. Explain in appropriate language what you plan to do and what the child may do.
9. Avoid prescribing the child's images or pain perceptions. Although it is incorrect to say that something will not hurt, it is also incorrect to say that something will hurt. The doctor or nurse can say, "Some children say this feels like cold ice, some say it feels like a thorn from a bush, and some say it feels like a cat scratching. I wonder what it will feel like for you."

There are many hypnotic techniques to teach children, depending on their age and preference. One approach is to offer the child a pretend "magical glove" to make your hand numb. The doctor or nurse then slowly puts on the pretend glove, finger by finger, encouraging the child to notice the numb feeling. A prior careful history will allow the doctor or nurse to know if, for example, the child had a previous "numbing" experience like another cut or a dental extraction, in which the memory of the absence of discomfort can be recalled and helpful in using the magic glove.

Another favorite approach is to explain about nerves going from all parts of the body to the brain. It helps to make a drawing of nerves from the legs, stomach, arms, and head. One can explain to a school-age child that it is impossible to pay attention to more than one or two body sensations at the same time, and that we are continually turning off our awareness to many of our nerves. Thus, we already know how to do this and the child can learn to voluntarily turn off body suggestions. The doctor or nurse can also ask the child to think about what might be a favorite type of switch, for example, flip switch, dimmer switch, pull switch, or push-button switch. The child can then practice turning off the switches that connect his brain to various areas of the body. This method is easily understood by most children and very effective.

Sometimes children like the analogy of one part of the body communicating with the brain by "imaginary cell phones" that allow, for example, a "sore part" to talk to the brain and ask for the switch to be turned off, or for the bladder to call the brain and tell the brain when it is full.

Chapter 6

Posttraumatic stress disorder (PTSD)

Eric Vermetten and Ciara Christensen

6.1 OVERVIEW OF POSTTRAUMATIC STRESS DISORDER (PTSD)

Human violence, including rape, robberies, assault, natural disaster, and accidents can leave the individual with intense terror, fear, and paralyzing helplessness. In the United States alone, about 60% of men and 50% of women have experienced psychological trauma (defined as threat to life of self or significant other) at some time in their lives. Unfortunately, these percentages are larger in developing countries where individuals are exposed to multiple traumatic events.

PTSD is defined as a mental disorder characterized by a preoccupation with traumatic events beyond normal human experience. Events such as rape or personal assault, combat, violence against civilians, natural disasters, accidents or torture precipitate this mental disorder. Patients suffer from recurring flashbacks of the trauma and often feel emotionally numb; are overly alert; have difficulty remembering, sleeping, or concentrating; and may feel guilty for surviving.

6.2 DIAGNOSTIC CATEGORIES

Symptoms of PTSD are divided into three categories: (a) re-experiencing event, (b) avoidance of stimuli, and (c) persistent symptoms of increased arousal. The symptoms must lead to social and functional impairments and must be present for 3 months in order to meet the diagnostic threshold (American Psychiatric Association, 2000).

Symptoms of PTSD generally become evident within the first months following the trauma; sometimes acute stress disorder (ASD) develops into PTSD. ASD may occur immediately after traumatic stress exposure. It may last from 2 days to 4 weeks and includes symptoms of dissociation, such as derealization and depersonalization. In many individuals, PTSD can be a chronic disorder that they take with them to their graves, putting a burden on physical and mental health, and on health providers.

A close relationship exists between PTSD, dissociation, somatization, and a variety of other problems (Bower & Sivers, 1998; Bremmer, 2002; Butler, Duran, Jasiukaitis, Koopman, & Spiegel, 1996; Cahill, 1997; van der Kolk, Pelcovitz, et al., 1996; Vermetten, Dorahy, & Spiegel, 2007). Chronic interpersonal trauma, especially with a childhood onset such as incest, physical abuse, torture, or neglect, can lead to a much broader range of symptoms, described as complex PTSD.

There may also be the experience of profound feelings of guilt and the feeling of blaming oneself for surviving when others did not, keeping the guilt inside. This conflict, in its most acute presentation, typically resembles an agitated depression and is described as being associated with frequent dreams of friends dying (e.g., in battle) and by avoidance of interpersonal intimacy because of the fear the other party may abandon them or die.

PTSD is also frequently comorbid with other psychiatric disorders, such as depression, substance abuse, and anxiety disorders (Kessler, Sonnega, Bromet, Hughes, & Nelson, 1995). Clinicians assessing victims of chronic interpersonal trauma need to be particularly aware that the presentation may very well include many other problems than the core symptoms of PTSD. Comorbidity may also reflect a more general vulnerability to psychopathology that renders some individuals more susceptible to developing a variety of disorders, including PTSD (Weathers, Ruscio, & Keane, 1999).

PTSD can result from a single type trauma, sometimes referred to as type I trauma (rape, assault) or from repetitive, chronic trauma exposure, referred to as type II trauma (child abuse, war). Its onset can be early in life or later as an adult. This has important consequences for therapy. In early life trauma, the psychopathology is usually complex.

6.3 ASSESSMENT

Trauma measures vary widely in scope and format, ranging from self-report checklists assessing the presence or absence of a limited range of potentially traumatic events to comprehensive protocols assessing a wide range of stressors through both self-report and interview.

The caveat for the diagnosis of PTSD is nondisclosure (not talking about the trauma out of reasons of shame, guilt, fear of prosecution). Clinicians also need to be aware of overreporting of symptoms in those with secondary gain opportunities.

6.4 TREATMENT

Control, rapport, and history are key elements in the treatment of patients with PTSD. Patients have no difficulty in remembering and overengaging in the traumatic scene; they need to be able to resolve the underlying issues through hypnotic abreactive or adjunctive alternative hypnotic interventions. Such resolution restructures the patient's personality to function more adaptively.

Given the different clusters of PTSD symptoms, the practitioner may find only partial response in individual patients with a single medication and will find it necessary to consider addressing the multiple symptoms with a combination of medications.

Antidepressant medications are the mainstay of treatment. The timing of prescribing medication is also an important issue; in a phase-oriented approach for PTSD using hypnosis, the medication should enhance and not interfere with the effect of hypnotherapy.

6.5 PTSD AND HYPNOSIS

PTSD patients as a group are moderately high in hypnotizability (Bryant, Guthrie, Moulds, Nixon, & Felmingham, 2003; Spiegel, Hunt, & Dondershine, 1988). The application of psychotherapeutic interventions should use this capacity. For example, hypnosis has been shown to have a significant additive benefit to cognitive-behavioral therapy for ASD and PTSD (Bryant, Guthrie, Moulds, & Nixon, 2005).

Traumatic experiences can mobilize hypnotic responses (spontaneous hypnotic state; Barabasz, 2005–2006) during which intense absorption in the hypnotic focal experience can be achieved by means of a dissociation of experience (Nijenhuis, Spinhoven, van Dyck, van der Hart, & Vanderlinden, 1998).

Subsequent reactivation of traumatic memories can also have trancelike features: the attention of the individual is captured, there is a general loss of orientation in time and space, and experiences are processed in a dissociated way (e.g., painful sensory stimulation does not necessarily require analgesia). These traumatic memories could well be considered a specific subgroup of fear-related emotional memories.

One of the most intriguing aspects of trauma disorders is the re-experiencing phenomena. Numerous labels and descriptions have been applied to this phenomenon. Traumatic recall is also referred to as a flashback, which typically involves the reliving of the traumatic event with strong emotional involvement. Flashbacks can lead to sleeping problems, irritability, feeling worse with traumatic reminders, and secondary avoidance.

Neuroimaging has shed a light on the retrieval aspect of memory and its emotional involvement by investigating brain processes that occur during traumatic recall (Vermetten & Bremner, 2004; Vermetten & Spiegel, 2007). In PTSD patients, traumatic cues, such as a particular sight or sound reminiscent of the original traumatic event, typically can induce a cascade of anxiety and fear-related symptoms, sometimes without conscious recall of the original traumatic event.

The traumatic stimulus may not always be easy to identify; it may be through exposure to a movie, a smell, or, more subtle, a gesture or voice, that a memory is metaphorically reawakened. Traumatic memories can remain indelible for years or decades and can be activated by a variety of stimuli and stressors. A model of extinction to explain this does not seem to qualify in these cases; a better model seems to be the failure of successful inhibition of traumatic memories (van der Kolk, 1994).

There are a number of emotional states that characterize PTSD in addition to exaggerated fear responses to threat. As reviewed earlier, these include symptoms of dissociation, loss of self-agency, feeling worse with traumatic reminders, amnesia, and flashbacks upon visual imagery of the traumatic event that plays back like a movie.

Hypnosis is thought of as controlled dissociation, and dissociation, in turn, as a form of spontaneous self-hypnosis The notion that parts of the body that previously experienced physical disease of trauma seem to be especially vulnerable to reactivation of that response with hypnosis (Spiegel & Vermetten, 2007) requires identification of underlying mechanisms that can subsequently be integrated into a broader neurobiology knowledge base. Reciprocally, when these mechanisms are compatible with mainstream explanatory neurobiological circuits and systems, they may contribute to a shift in the body of established medical theory by emphasizing previously neglected factors (cf. Rainville & Price, 2003).

6.6 PSYCHOLOGICAL TREATMENT OF PTSD USING HYPNOSIS

Hypnotic treatment allows modifying ownership and agency of traumatic memories. All interventions in the following paragraph are language based and involve attention, imagination, and engagement in mind processes while they center on modulation of affective/fear-driven responses. Hypnosis in treatment of PTSD is often embedded in a phase-oriented approach in which three elements need to be timed sequentially:

1. Symptom stabilization—Relaxation-based anxiety management, without medication
2. Exposure—Working through the trauma, abreaction, and alternatives to abreaction
3. Closure—Usually with ritual, providing a perspective (Horowitz, 1986)

6.7 HYPNOSIS FOR RELEASE OF UNBOUND AFFECT

Patients respond pathologically when faced with what they construe as a trip wire reminder associated with previous traumatic stress. Unresolved trauma will produce unwanted symptoms. Hypnosis, particularly when used as part of ego state therapy (Watkins & Barabasz, 2008), targets PTSD by allowing the fullest expression by the traumatized ego state, while providing the needed recourse to respond to the threatening agent.

Once resolved in this brief therapy, the symptoms of PTSD disappear because they are no longer driven by the underlying state that carried the unresolved trauma. The patient has overcome the fear and can quickly return to normal range functioning, adaptive, at ease, and empowered. Thus, hypnosis is a powerful contribution to the treatment of PTSD, which makes it the treatment of choice for experienced clinicians (Lynn & Cardena, 2007; Spiegel, 1992). Hypnosis is a catalyst for emotional catharsis as a form of release therapy. As explained by Watkins and Barabasz (2008, pp. 57–58), hypnosis can facilitate the revivification of emotionally disturbing experiences that happened to the individual and can release the affect that has been connected to that experience. When skillfully carried out, the result can produce a feeling of relief to the patient and disappearance of the patient's psychopathology related to that experience. Perhaps the most powerful contribution of hypnosis to the treatment of PTSD, which makes it the treatment of choice for experienced clinicians, is the ability of hypnosis to facilitate emotional catharsis as a form of release therapy.

Ego state therapy is a comprehensive therapy that is particularly appropriate for PTSD. It incorporates hypnotic abreaction, affect, resistance bridge techniques, and other procedures to produce a resilient adaptive restructuring of the personality. Research, thus far, consistently supports ego state therapy as superior to cognitive-behavior therapy (Emmerson, 2003; Paulson, 2007; Watkins & Barabasz, 2008; Watkins & Watkins, 1997).

Additional procedures to facilitate release of unbound affect include

1. Slow release/slow burn procedure—The abreaction can be accomplished in a piecemeal fashion with noticeable and sometimes remarkable advances during each session (see Watkins & Barabasz, 2008, pp. 90–91).
2. Kluft's fractionated abreaction—This technique involves bringing the emotionally laden material to awareness gradually through a variety of uncovering techniques involving the feelings associated with the memory to emerge in "solitary moments." Hypnotic time distortion is used to help the affect emerge with lower intensity but over a much longer duration of time (Kluft, 1986, 1992).

3. The split screen technique—This hypnotic technique is projective in nature in that it implies that the patient will "project sensations, images, and thoughts onto an imaginary screen of the patient's choosing" (e.g., computer screen, surface of a calm lake, a clear blue sky). It is intended to separate the painful sensations and thus attenuate traumatic abreaction as may be encountered in the reconstruction of traumatic early memories (Spiegel & Spiegel, 2004). As described by Watkins and Barabasz (2008), patients learn they can control the intensity of content by adjusting the size or color of the images or the proximity to the screen. Patients can also turn the screen off if the image of the memory becomes too overwhelming. A variation of the technique, also developed by the Spiegels, asks the patient to divide the screen. The patient can project a left sinister side, that is the trauma side, and then on the right side a picture of how they could protect themselves and stand up to the perpetrator or perpetrators or otherwise adaptively handle the abuser or the incident.

4. Eye movement desensitization and reprocessing (EMDR)— EMDR is a psychotherapeutic approach that involves what experts in the field of hypnosis view as a specific hypnotic induction (Spiegel, 2007). It has received status as evidence-based medicine (EBM) via the U.S. Department of Veterans Affairs/Department of Defense Clinical Practice Guidelines, the Northern Ireland Department of Health, the Israeli National Council for Mental Health, Division 12 of the American Psychological Association, and the International Society for Traumatic Stress Studies (see Silver, Rogers, Knipe, & Colelli, 2005). In addition to the hypnotic induction aspect, it also combines elements of psychodynamic, cognitive-behavioral, physiological, and interactional therapies (Shapiro, 2002). The theory asserts that memories may be eradicated when fully processed through the use of carefully timed bilateral stimulation. The eye movement method is the preferred technique by the majority of experienced EMDR clinicians and trainers (Milstein, 2007). Alternatives include both auditory tones and tactile stimulation. Trauma reactive memory networks are viewed as the underlying basis of pathology and mental health that may be responsive to EMDR (see van der Kolk, 2007). As found in rigorously controlled research

on the hypnotic state, using Positron Emission Tomography (PET) (Kosslyn, Thompson, Constantine-Ferrando, Alpert, & Spiegel, 2000) hyperactivation of the related brain regions are found during EMDR eye movement induction (Levin, Lazrove, & van der Kolk, 1999). EMDR goals include (a) resolution of memories; (b) desensitization of stimuli that trigger present distress as a result of second-order conditioning; and (c) incorporation of adaptive attitudes, skills, and behaviors. Experienced EMDR trainers are almost universally trained in hypnosis and view EMDR as within the domain of hypnosis (Paulson, 2007). EMDR avoids full abreactive expression in favor of "containment." Containment facilitated by statements such as "that's just old stuff" may be attractive to less skilled therapists who cannot handle the intensity of a full-blown abreaction, as is typically the goal in brief hypnotic ego state therapy (EST). EST, therefore, when properly carried out to full resolution and with subsequent supportive grounding while still in hypnosis, can be expected to produce a long-lasting curative effect superior to EMDR.

6.8 CONCLUSIONS

The role of hypnosis in traumatic recall is a caveat and at the same time a promise for patients with trauma-related disorders. Traumatized individuals, with trauma-related psychopathology like PTSD or other trauma-related disorders, can alternate among states of consciousness. In most cases, they experience their trauma over and over again as if it were happening on the spot. These events are often experienced with the same vividness and psychophysiologic changes and episodes in which they were encoded.

This is a population that has been shown to be generally highly hypnotizable. Those with PTSD can use their hypnotic capacity to block pain, alter time perception, or modify their affective response in a situation of traumatic recall. The challenge for a patient is to learn to control the spontaneous hypnotic disposition by means of psychotherapeutic interventions that address self-hypnosis and are embedded in a stepwise/graded program of release of unbound affect, symptom stabilization, exposure, and closure.

Figure 6.1 Dr. Barabasz and Ciara Christensen demonstrate hypnotic abreactions (from Watkins & Barabasz, 2008).

Alert hypnosis induced, painting of perpetrator begins

Abreaction begins

Figure 6.2 Ciara Christensen demonstrates the hypnographic technique for abreaction (from Watkins & Barabasz, 2008).

Abreaction near exhaustion, the point the practitioner becomes
reinvolved to provide reassurance and personality reconstruction

Figure 6.2 (continued)

Chapter 7

Surgery

Linda Thomson

7.1 INTRODUCTION: USING HYPNOSIS BEFORE SURGERY

Millions of minor and major surgical operations and invasive interventional medical procedures are performed each year around the world. Preparing patients hypnotically for surgery can have an enormous positive impact on both their surgical course and their recovery. Hypnosis can be very effective in enhancing the patient's coping skills, managing stress and anxiety, reducing pain, and increasing a sense of self-mastery in the patient having surgery.

7.2 WHAT THE RESEARCH HAS SHOWN

Hypnosis can be used as a sole anesthetic for patients with above average hypnotizability (Barabasz & Watkins, 2005), but most often hypnosis is used to potentiate the effects of analgesics and anesthetics, facilitate postoperative healing, and to help maintain stability of vital signs. A review of 18 studies looking at the effects of presurgical psychological interventions (hypnosis, suggestion and relaxation) revealed that patients who are psychologically prepared for surgery have shorter hospital stays, have less postoperative pain and use fewer narcotics, have decreased anxiety, less nausea and vomiting, and earlier return of gastrointestinal (GI) function (Blankfield, 1991). In the following decade, there was a meta-analysis looking at just the beneficial impact of adjunctive hypnosis with surgical patients (Montgomery, David, Winkel, Silverstein, & Bovbjerg, 2002). It found that patients in the hypnosis groups had outcomes better than 89% of the patients in control groups.

The use of nonpharmacologic interventions during invasive vascular and renal procedures was studied by Lang et al. (2000). Patients in the hypnosis group of this randomized, controlled study were found to have less pain and anxiety than the control group, despite the use of less analgesics and anxiolytics. Further research went on to show a cost savings of $338 per patient in the hypnosis group. This was felt in large part to be due to their greater hemodynamic stability (Lang & Rosen, 2002). Other researchers have found significantly less nausea and vomiting following surgery when hypnosis was used. A randomized, controlled study by Ginandes (2003) showed faster wound healing and improved functional recovery in women following breast surgery. Presurgical hypnosis has been shown to significantly reduce bleeding during spine surgery. Bennett (1993) showed that hypnosis, not relaxation or suggestion alone, was more effective in improving postsurgical healing times.

7.3 OBTAINING THE HISTORY

Hypnosis can be used preoperatively, intraoperatively, and postoperatively (Barabasz & Watkins, 2005). A careful history should be obtained by the clinician while building rapport with the patient. It is important to determine the what, where, when, and why of the surgery along with the expected postoperative course.

Previous experience with hospitalizations, surgery, and hypnosis should be established as well as the patient's particular thoughts, wishes, worries, and fears. It is always important to determine how the patient's life will be better after the surgery so that this can be reflected back in trance.

The person's spiritual belief system is also important. The patient may request scripture, prayer, or a poem with special meaning be included in the trance work. The building of the therapeutic alliance between patient and practitioner can reduce anxiety and facilitate acceptance of the hypnotic intervention, thus leading ideally to a successful surgical outcome.

7.4 TRANCEWORK

The careful use of language is essential when working hypnotically with a surgical patient. Electroencephalograph (EEG) event-related potentials have shown that the structure of hypnotic suggestions can be crucial (Barabasz et al., 1999).

For most children and adults, having surgery creates both pain and anxiety. Feelings of helplessness and dependency create fear and frustration. Individuals often feel they have lost control of the situation. The nocebo response is the antithesis of the placebo response. Patients with a negative expectancy are more likely to have a negative outcome. Through the careful use of language, hypnosis can control for the nocebo response. Hypnosis uses language to create a new paradigm.

There is, perhaps, no use for hypnosis where the careful use of language is more important than when hypnosis is used for surgical patients (Thomson, 2005). Statements like "you will be put to sleep" or "it's all over" need to be reworded so the statement does not have an implicit suggestion.

The practitioner can use hypnosis to reframe the entire surgical experience for the patient. Hypnotic intervention returns to the patient the sense of mastery by enhancing his or her perception of control and ability.

Hypnotic interventions therapy can produce helpful perceptual changes in the pain experience by suggestions for movement or displacement of pain, amnesia for pain, and altering anticipation. Hypnotic techniques of time distortion may be used to lengthen the interval between pains and shorten the duration of pain. Distraction, shifting the attention to an external focus, or internal distraction involving mental work can be useful.

Surgery is a traumatic injury that stimulates the stress response. Stress delays healing and surgical recovery (Glaser et al., 1999). Hypnosis can mitigate that response. With hypnosis, the relaxation response can be substituted for the stress response.

The following can be used as a framework around which to create a script for a surgery patient that is adjusted and personalized to meet the patient's individual needs. The induction would depend on the individual's previous experience with hypnosis, ease of relaxing, anxiety level, and rapport.

To establish a low stress, low anxiety environment, a safe place of comfort needs to be created. This would be a safe place that the patient can return to in his imagination whenever he wants or needs to. A patient should be offered a technique for getting rid of unwanted thoughts or worries, such as floating them off on a cloud. As the patient awaits surgery in the operating room and preoperative area, there will be many interruptions that can be utilized for fractionation to take the patient deeper into trance. After induction of hypnosis, one suggestion might be:

> You will be interested to note that as you are asked to answer questions or are asked to do anything, that it does not disrupt your level of comfort. In fact anytime during your journey that you open your eyes or are asked to move from one place to another, you will notice when you close your eyes again, you will feel yourself becoming even more deeply relaxed.

With children, eyes-open, alert hypnosis can be used because they enter the hypnotic state best by active engagement and are typically reluctant to close their eyes during medical intervention.

Not everything the patient hears in the operating room and preoperatively will be therapeutic or even pertain to the patient. This hypnotic suggestion may be given:

> Pay attention only to the voice that is speaking directly to you. All other sounds will seem pleasantly far away. And if anyone says anything to you that is less than helpful, it will be as if they are speaking in a foreign language that you do not understand.

Since operating rooms are kept cool, suggestions for warmth or a healing light are useful. The high tech equipment in hospitals and operating rooms can be quite frightening. The patient may be given the suggestion that

> the equipment is all there to help your surgery go well and perhaps you will notice how safe it makes you feel.

Aspects of medical stability and healing need to be addressed. Hemodynamic stability can be enhanced with a hypnotic suggestion that as the operative area is being washed with the antiseptic solution, it will be a signal to constrict the blood vessels to that area diverting blood flow to all other areas. Suggestions concerning homeostasis are given.

> Your inner mind knows how to regulate your blood flow, blood pressure and blood glucose at the level that is perfect for you.

The patient will find it especially reassuring to hear in hypnosis:

> Your doctor and nurses will take good care of you, but know also that you can do anything you need to do to increase your level of comfort. When your procedure is over, the healing can begin immediately.

To enhance postoperative pain control, this hypnotic suggestion can be given:

> The sensations that you feel will be those of healing and mending and need not bother you.

Earlier return of GI function and decreased postoperative vomiting can be accomplished with the following suggestions:

> Note with pleasure how soon all of your bodily functions return to normal. You will swallow to clear your throat and that will be the signal to your digestive track—one way going down, only going down.

Hypnotic suggestions to enhance healing might include

> You can look forward to feeling better, getting better so you can enjoy life fully. As your body heals, different changes occur and you can cooperate with the work of your body by remaining as calm as you are now. Your only responsibility is for healing. Everything else is being taken care of. There are no demands on you and no expectations. At any time during your recovery period you can go right back to this place of comfort and relaxation.

The patient may be offered amnesia for the uncomfortable portions of the procedure and ego strengthening for their hypnotic success:

> You may choose to remember to forget or forget to remember as much or as little of this experience as you want or need to. You will remember to remember that you were able to give yourself an amazing amount of comfort.

7.5 SUMMARY

The practitioner skilled in hypnosis has the wonderful opportunity to use this powerful modality with patients who are facing surgery. The patients will be significantly more relaxed, experience greater comfort, and have faster healing than those who are not hypnotically prepared. With hypnotic interventions, the patient is empowered to take charge of his or her recovery. Postoperative recovery time will be reduced with subsequent cost savings while the probability of patient satisfaction is maximized.

Chapter 8

Childbirth

Jacqueline M. Irland

8.1 INTRODUCTION: SELF-HYPNOSIS FOR CHILDBIRTH

Childbirth is one of the most profound events a woman and couple will experience. Unfortunately, the experience can be fraught with anxiety, as well as fear of pain and loss of control. Often during childbirth, a woman engages a fight-or-flight response, which increases her perception of pain intensity and decreases internal blood flow. Armed with the ability to use self-hypnotic techniques, women and their partners can effectively enter the childbirth experience with calm and focus (Barabasz & Watkins, 2005, pp. 257–288; McCarthy, 2001; Oster, 1994, 2000).

Self-hypnosis helps women disengage the sympathetic fight-or-flight response, impacting the birthing process and their perception of the experience. When internal blood flow is optimal, there is also increased uterine blood flow and increased oxygen perfusion through the placenta. In areas where epidural analgesia is unavailable or in maternal conditions where it is contraindicated (e.g., thrombocytopenia or low platelets), self-hypnosis is an alternative that provides increased comfort during childbirth with decreased maternal risk.

There are few studies providing guidelines for childbirth hypnosis and expected outcomes (Brown & Hammond, 2007; Cyna, Andrew, & McAuliffe, 2006; Harmon, Hynan, & Tyre, 1990; Letts, Baker, Ruderman, & Kennedy, 1993; Mehl-Madrona, 2004). Most published articles provide anecdotal reports or summaries. More rigorous, evidence-based studies are indeed necessary.

From my experience of teaching more than 300 couples over the past 7 years, the following suggested format has been successful with both individual couples and groups preparing for childbirth.

Although the results are almost always therapeutic, teaching a skill set is the overall goal of a self-hypnosis for childbirth programs. Hypnotizability testing is unnecessary prior to working with a woman or couple. Motivation seems to be the greatest predictor of success during childbirth, and consistent practice between training sessions eliminates the differences attributed to individual variations in hypnotizability. This is, however, counter to the practice and experience of a number of other practitioners (McCarthy, 1998; Harmon et al., 1990). The specific effects of pregnancy ("the pregnant brain"; DeAngelis, 2008) on hypnotizability have yet to be studied.

The specific skills needed for childbirth include self-induction for the woman, resting techniques, pain management, using several sensory options for focus, techniques to deal with external distractions, development of birthing metaphors, and helping skills for her partner. Because the process of childbirth involves radical changes in the intensity and frequency of pain stimuli, varying lengths of labor, and multiple external interruptions by devices and caregivers, many traditional hypnotic approaches are unsuccessful in preparing women for this challenge.

For example, only a handful of women I interviewed immediately after giving birth reported that hypnotic techniques totally eliminated their perception of contraction pain. The vast majority testified, however, that the success of hypnosis was related to decreased anxiety; their perception that they were engaged in a birthing adventure; the continual presence of a partner or caregiver who provided comfort, safety, and focus; and their ability to rest and calm themselves. This was especially important for women who had previous birthing experiences without the use of self-hypnosis. It is therefore important to teach women and their partners skills that address all of the aforementioned concerns if their use of self-hypnosis is to be successful.

8.2 CHILDBIRTH AS AN ADVENTURE

Childbirth can be approached as a painful obstacle to be overcome or as a journey to be traveled and experienced, using all the skills and options available. The metaphor of a childbirth adventure conjures feelings of excitement and curiosity. Hypnosis provides an opportunity for women or a couple to prepare for an adventure where they know what the destination will be but they are not certain of how they will reach it.

Because contractions come and go as do waves, hills, and gusts of wind, these often provide the most useful metaphors for childbirth (Barabasz & Watkins, 2005, pp. 276–284; McCarthy, 1998; Mehl-Madrona, 2004). The laboring woman may find herself working intensely through her contractions, or moving away from the physical sensations to a distant image, a sound, or a tactile sensation. Alternative and commonly used protocols using the "adventure" theme have been tested with more than 600 cases (Barabasz & Watkins, 2005). When the woman is given, however, the opportunity and encouragement, through discussion and in trance, she will often develop her own metaphors that are much more creative and personal, and will serve her even more effectively during her journey.

The most important skill she must develop for this journey is, however, the ability to rest deeply between the contractions. This should become an automatic response to moving over the peak of a contraction, as the intensity decreases and she can rest. For most women it is necessary to work when moving over a contraction. They are encouraged to see, hear, or feel the peak ahead of them and begin to rest as they move down the other side as if they were coasting down a hill on a bike or over a wave.

The adventure becomes one of ever-increasing waves, hills, and gusts of wind. She works over each of these becoming more confident and adept at moving up to the top and resting as she moves over the peaks and down the other side. This experience is more successful if she is accompanied by a partner or caregiver who provides companionship, comfort, and safety.

8.3 THE CHILDBIRTH PARTNER

Traditionally, only the client or patient who must deal with a painful physical experience is taught hypnotic techniques. Because the woman is awake and alert during childbirth, there is often a partner who is invested in the journey, and there are often multiple other caregivers involved. Teaching a childbirth partner to use and reinforce hypnotic skills is important (Oster, 1994, 2000). This partner can be a spouse, friend, family member, or medical caregiver. The partner's role is to protect, mediate, calm, soothe, and provide focus, allowing the laboring woman to do her important internal work without fear of journeying alone or of a sudden intrusion from outside. If possible, partners are taught self-hypnosis techniques for their own use and to better understand the needs of the laboring woman. They are given instructions out of trance and suggestions in trance to help them fulfill their role.

I have found no difference in the success of male versus female birthing partners. Motivation of the partner and trust between the woman and her partner are the most important variables. The process of learning the skill of self-hypnosis as a team builds and enhances this motivation and trust.

8.4 PAIN MANAGEMENT

In most cases, the pain of labor contractions is not a constant pain. Anxiety and fear of pain and loss of control can, however, cause the perception that the contraction pain never subsides. In the context of a hypnotic childbirth adventure, discomfort and the unknown become part of the intrigue and are more easily managed without anxiety. It is important that the woman learns and practices several options for working with the discomfort of contractions.

Self-hypnosis practice with pain simulation should be provided in the same manner that contractions occur. Contractions occur for approximately 1 minute with resting between contractions for 2 to 3 minutes. To simulate contractions, the partner can apply ice to both of the woman's wrists or pinch the area of her hand between her forefinger and thumb for 1 minute followed by 2 to 3 minutes of rest.

While using self-hypnosis, images, sounds, and feelings of working through the sensations or moving away can be suggested, followed by hypnotic suggestions of deep rest and soothing when the stimulus is removed. Ice and pinching work well because these can be easily practiced away from training sessions.

During self-hypnosis practice, instruments such as hemostats and needles should not be used because they can cause damage to tissue and increase the woman's anxiety regarding the possible use of these during childbirth. Following any simulation, the partners should be encouraged to share with each other their experiences. This enhances their experience of teamwork and the communication that should be occurring during their adventure together.

8.5 VARIATIONS IN SENSORY PREFERENCES

With the multitude of interruptions that can occur during child-birth, the success of using hypnosis can be greatly enhanced when women have access to many options for sensory focus. Women may be more attuned to one or more types of visual, auditory, or tactile stimuli. Offering these during her hypnosis training and encouraging her to experiment on her own with different stimuli helps to broaden her options for focus during her childbirth adventure. Her partner should also be sensitive to the sensory language that will be most helpful to her. All of the following can be woven into her hypnosis training and practice. Recordings of waves, rivers or streams, storms, and rain can be used to induce and deepen her trance during practice sessions and childbirth. Marbles or stones, cloth textures, and clay or play dough work well as options for tactile focus. Visual imagery, candles, and pictures are options for visual focus.

During childbirth most women are very sensitive to olfactory stimuli. Providing aromatherapy with elements such as lavender, mint, or many others depending on the woman's preferences may help calm or energize, while masking other odors that can interfere with her focus. If a woman is birthing away from home, she should also be encouraged to bring soothing items from home, such as her pillow, pictures, cloth pieces, and so forth.

8.6 HYPNOSIS FOR OPERATIVE CHILDBIRTH

Cesarean childbirth is unfortunately becoming more common. For many women this provokes increased anxiety and fear of loss of control. This anxiety may impact the sympathetic nervous system to such a degree that the woman's vital signs become erratic and regional anesthetic (epidural or spinal) may be less effective for her cesarean birth.

The use of hypnosis during a cesarean can provide a focus distant from the operative environment and help a woman to feel safe and calm. Again the goal is to teach a skill set that will enable the woman to comfort and soothe herself while providing increased blood flow internally to her uterus and oxygen to her baby. This way she decreases her sympathetic response to this experience.

8.7 WORKING WITH VARYING CULTURES AND RELIGIOUS BELIEFS

Working with individuals of other backgrounds rather than women and couples of European descent, it seems that prayer and deep spiritual beliefs can often play an important role. In these individuals there seems to be a much more open response to the physical, mental, and emotional changes that accompany the trance experience. I often hear from such individuals that they have experienced trance phenomena during their activities of meditation, or individual or group prayer. Introducing self-hypnosis for childbirth as another type of very focused mental activity works well to demystify its use and provide women or a couple with a comfortable background from which to begin their practice of self-hypnosis for childbirth.

8.9 CONCLUSIONS

The success of hypnosis in childbirth is related to decreased anxiety, reduction of time in the first stage of labor, reduction or elimination of pain, decreased shock, more rapid recovery, lowered incidence of operative delivery, facilitation of decreased anesthesia of the perineum, delivery, episiotomy, and suturing. Thus, hypnosis produces a positive perception of the birthing adventure, with the continual presence of a partner to provide comfort and safety, and the ability to rest deeply between contractions. The hypnotic approach described in this chapter draws from the experience and writings of many practitioners, it also differs from many previous approaches. The primary differences are the inclusion of a partner in all aspects of self-hypnosis training, the lack of emphasis on hypnotizability, increased emphasis on autonomic nervous system effects, and the development of personal childbirth metaphors.

Chapter 9

Hypnosis and sleep

Michael Yapko

9.1 INTRODUCTION

This brief chapter will focus specifically on how hypnosis can help resolve insomnia that is secondary to depression. Depression is the most common mood disorder in the world and, according to the World Health Organization (2001), is a leading cause of human suffering and disability that is still increasing in prevalence. Insomnia is the most common sleep disorder related to depression. Insomnia is defined as: "A complaint of difficulty initiating sleep, maintaining sleep, and/or non-restorative sleep that causes clinically significant distress or impairment in social, occupational, or other important areas of functioning" (Littner et al., 2003, p. 754). Thus, an individual may complain of having difficulty initially falling asleep or staying asleep, the latter condition manifesting as either middle-of-the-night or early morning awakenings.

The negative consequences of chronic insomnia are substantial. Occupationally, these include a higher rate of absenteeism from work, greater use of health services, a higher number of accidents, and decreased productivity. On a personal level, chronic insomnia sufferers report a decreased quality of life, loss of memory functions, feeling fatigued, unable to concentrate well, and diminished interest in socializing or engaging in pleasurable activities, further increasing depressive symptoms. A sleep disturbance can increase the risk for alcohol-related problems. Survey respondents who reported sleep disturbances more than 12 years later had twice as high a rate of alcohol-related problems (Crum, Storr, Chan, & Ford, 2004).

9.2 INSOMNIA AS A RISK FACTOR FOR DEPRESSION

Because insomnia and depression are so often found together, it is logical to wonder whether insomnia causes depression, depression causes insomnia, or whether they cause each other. The best evidence to date suggests that insomnia and depression share some common pathology that leads to both conditions (Ford & Kamerow, 1989; Thase, 2000).

The onset of insomnia may serve as an "early warning signal" for an impending depressive episode and thus may be considered a significant risk factor for the eventual development of depression. There may be a fourfold increase in the relative risk of developing major depression when people have a history of insomnia. Insomnia more often precedes the onset of a first episode of depression (Thase, 2000).

Thus, an early diagnosis of insomnia may afford clinicians an opportunity to prevent depression's onset if it is recognized and treated appropriately. Unfortunately, only about 33% of those suffering insomnia report it to their physicians, and only about 5% of those with insomnia actively seek treatment for it (Cochran, 2003). Thus, both depression and insomnia are underreported and underdiagnosed problems.

9.3 TREATMENT OPTIONS FOR DEPRESSION-RELATED INSOMNIA

Interventions currently in use for treating depression-related insomnia fall into two general categories: medications and psychotherapy. Self-help strategies, such as hypnosis, are a viable alternative. Unlike other self-help approaches, hypnosis is specifically cited for insomnia by the United States National Institutes of Health ("Integration," 1996) technology assessment panel.

The use of self-help techniques for enhancing sleep offers several key advantages: Self-help will not lead to either addiction or dependence, it can be applied under all conditions, and it will not lead to potentially harmful interactions with other interventions (Yapko, 2006).

9.4 HYPNOSIS AND PSYCHOTHERAPY FOR INSOMNIA

The use of hypnosis in treating insomnia and sleep disturbances has been described in numerous clinical reports, such as those of Bauer and McCanne (1980), Becker (1993), Borkovec and Fowles (1973), and Koe (1989). Some articles describe the successful use of hypnosis for anxiety reduction, relaxation, and the use of thought slowing and redirection. One study reported successful use of a hypnotic relaxation technique, compared to a stimulus control and placebo, for reducing late sleep onset (Stanton, 1989).

Hypnosis may be of greatest benefit in psychotherapy when it is used as a means of teaching skills that empower the client. There are specific skills that someone suffering insomnia can learn that will make a positive difference. These skills include: relaxation, good sleep hygiene, and ameliorating rumination. Rumination is the cognitive process of spinning around the same thoughts over and over again. It is considered an enduring style of coping with ongoing problems and stress that can both lead to and increase depression (Nolen-Hoeksema, 1991).

Coping responses may distinguish between strategies oriented toward confronting the problem and strategies oriented toward reducing tension by avoiding dealing with the problem directly. Rumination can be thought of as a pattern of avoidance that actually increases anxiety and agitation. Ruminative responses include repeatedly expressing to others how badly one feels, thinking to excess why one feels bad, and catastrophizing the negative effects of feeling bad. By ruminating, the person avoids having to take decisive and timely action, further compounding a personal sense of inadequacy.

Rumination leads to more negative interpretations of life events, greater recall of negative autobiographical memories and events, impaired problem-solving, and a reduced willingness to participate in pleasant activities. Various studies provide evidence that ruminative behavior is not only highly associated with depression, but serves to increase both the severity and duration of episodes of depression (Just & Alloy, 1997; Spasojevic & Alloy, 2001). Thus, rumination is an especially high priority target at which to aim interventions, hypnotic or otherwise.

Rumination generates both somatic and cognitive arousal, both of which can increase insomnia, but the evidence suggests cognitive arousal is the greater problem. Minimal cognitive processing and special effort toward sleep are key treatment goals.

9.5 HYPNOSIS, TARGETING RUMINATION, AND ENHANCING SLEEP

Hypnosis can teach the ability to direct one's own thoughts rather than merely react to them. This is a well-established dynamic and a principal reason for employing hypnosis in any context. Reducing the stressful wanderings of an agitated mind and also relaxing the body while simultaneously helping people create and follow a line of pleasant thoughts and images that can soothe and calm the person are valuable goals in the service of enhancing sleep.

To achieve these aims, there are a number of important components to include in one's treatment plan. These include

1. Teaching the client how to efficiently distinguish between useful analysis and useless ruminations. The distinction features variations in factors such as how much information to gather and how long to contemplate what to do. The single most important distinguishing characteristic is the conversion from analysis to action.
2. Enhancing skills in "time organization" (compartmentalization) to better separate bedtime from problem-solving time with the well-defined goal in place of keeping them separate.
3. Establishing better coping skills that involve more direct and effective problem-solving strategies. For example, the client that avoids making decisions or implements them out of the fear of making a mistake can be taught to make sensible and effective and, sometimes imperfect, problem-solving decisions.
4. Helping the client develop effective strategies for choosing among a range of alternatives. There is evidence that having more options, an oft-stated goal for clinicians, actually increases the anxiety and depression of those who don't have a good strategy for choosing among many alternatives.
5. Addressing issues of sleep hygiene and attitudes toward sleep to make sure the person's behavior and attitudes are consistent with good sleep. The fear of not being able to fall asleep

arouses anxiety and can impair sleep; likewise, if the physical environment is not conducive to sleep (i.e., noisy, hot), sleep will be adversely affected (Thase, 2000).

6. Teaching "mind-clearing" or "mind-focusing" strategies, especially self-hypnosis strategies that help the person direct his or her thinking in utterly harmless directions.

Each of the first five components listed support the potential value of the sixth, the actual hypnosis strategy one employs to help calm the person to sleep.

9.6 HYPNOTIC APPROACHES

Hypnosis can be used as a vehicle for teaching the client effective ways to make distinctions between useful analysis and useless ruminations, self organize (compartmentalize) various aspects of experience, develop better coping skills, develop more effective decision-making strategies, and develop good behavioral and thought habits regarding sleep.

Such hypnosis sessions are quite different in their structure than a session designed specifically for the purpose of enhancing the ability to fall and stay asleep. The primary difference between a sleep session and a regular therapy session employing hypnosis is that hypnosis for sleep enhancement is designed to actually lead the client to fall asleep.

In standard therapy sessions involving hypnosis, the opposite is true: The clinician takes active steps to prevent the client from falling asleep during the session. It has been well established that hypnosis is not a sleep state, and that sleep learning is a myth (Hull, 1933/2002; Yapko, 2003). Thus, clinicians employing hypnosis encourage the client to become focused and relaxed, yet maintain a sufficient degree of alertness to be capable of participating in the session by listening and actively adapting the clinician's suggestions to his or her particular needs.

Another key difference between a hypnosis session for enhancing sleep and a standard therapy session is the role of the client during the process. In therapy, the client is an active participant in utilizing suggestion and integrating new perspectives into the client's life.

Relaxation may or may not be a part of the therapy process. In fact, some suggestions a clinician offers during hypnosis might even be anxiety provoking or challenging to the client's sense of comfort. Personal growth often means stepping outside one's comfort zone. In the sleep session, however, cognitive and somatic arousal is to be minimized, and so challenges to the client's beliefs (or expectations, role definition, or any other aspect a clinician might appropriately challenge) are precluded. The content of the strategy (e.g., progressive relaxation, imagery from a favorite place, recollection of a happy memory, creation of fantasy stories, counting sheep, etc.) is a secondary consideration. Thus, what specific hypnotic approach one uses is relatively unimportant. The primary consideration is that whatever the client focuses on, it needs to be something that reduces both physical (somatic) and cognitive arousal.

Approaches can be direct or indirect according to the client's response. Likewise, they can be content or process oriented, again depending on the client. Since sleep isn't something that can be commanded, an authoritarian style is generally counterproductive. A permissive style is both gentler and more consistent with an attitude of allowing sleep to occur instead of trying to force it to occur.

The use of recorded hypnotic approaches (i.e., tape recordings or compact disc recordings) can be a useful means of helping the client to develop the skills in focusing on calming suggestions. Generally, these should be considered a temporary help in the process so that the person is eventually able to fall and stay asleep independently using self-hypnosis. However, recordings pose no major or even minor hazards that warrant concern that they will be abused in some way, so there seems to be no good reason to push clients to stop using the recordings for as long as they find them helpful.

9.7 INDICATIONS AND CONTRAINDICATIONS

There are no known contraindications to teaching clients to focus and relax. However, it is important that the client understand that hypnosis is a valuable tool for relaxing and reducing ruminations.

The rest of the larger treatment plan involves learning self-organization skills (compartmentalization) that will support the use of hypnosis to make a more enduring contribution to enhancing sleep. The client needs to be able to place the hypnosis in the context of the overall therapeutic approach the clinician is using.

9.8 CONCLUSIONS

Hypnosis can be used as a vehicle for teaching the client effective ways to make distinctions between useful analysis and useless ruminations, compartmentalize various aspects of experience, develop better coping skills, develop more effective decision-making strategies, and develop good behavioral and thought habits regarding sleep. Thus, hypnosis has substantial potential benefit to individuals suffering with insomnia arising in association with emotional stressors.

Chapter 10

Depression

Assen Alladin

10.1 HYPNOSIS FOR MAJOR DEPRESSION

This chapter will focus on hypnotherapy for major depressive disorder (MDD). MDD is among one of the most common psychiatric disorders treated by physicians and psychologists. Although MDD can be treated successfully with costly antidepressant medication and psychotherapy, a significant number of depressives do not respond to these approaches (Moore & Bona, 2001). It is thus important for clinicians to continue to develop more effective treatments for depression. This chapter describes cognitive hypnotherapy, a multimodal treatment approach to depression that may be applicable to a wide range of people with depression.

Cognitive hypnotherapy combined with cognitive behavior therapy (CBT) demonstrates substantial benefits (Schoenberger, 2000). A 1995 meta-analysis of 18 studies comparing CBT with the same treatment supplemented by hypnosis found the mean effect size for hypnotherapy was larger than the nonhypnotic treatment with a variety of emotional disorders (Kirsch, Montgomery, & Sapirstein, 1995). More recently, comparison of the effects of CBT with cognitive hypnotherapy among 84 chronic depressives showed an additive effect of combining hypnosis with CBT (Alladin & Alibhai, 2007). The study met the American Psychological Association (APA) criteria for probably efficacious treatment for depression (Chambless & Hollon, 1998) and it provided empirical validation for integrating hypnosis with CBT in the management of depression.

10.2 DESCRIPTION OF MAJOR DEPRESSIVE DISORDER (MDD)

MDD (used interchangeably with depression in this chapter) is characterized by feelings of sadness, lack of interest in formerly enjoyable pursuits, sleep and appetite disturbance, sense of worthlessness, and thoughts of death and dying (Alladin, 2007). Depression is extremely disabling in terms of poor quality of life and disability (Pincus & Pettit, 2001) and 15% of people with depression commit suicide (Satcher, 2000).

Depression is on the increase (World Health Organization, 1998) and it is estimated that out of every 100 people, approximately 13 men and 21 women are likely to develop the disorder at some point in life (Kessler et al., 1994) and approximately one third of the population may suffer from mild depression at some point in their lives (Paykel & Priest, 1992).

The rate of major depression is so high that the World Health Organization (WHO) Global Burden of Disease Study ranked depression as the single most burdensome disease in the world in terms of total disability-adjusted life years among people in their middle years of life (Murray & Lopez, 1996). According to WHO (1998), by the year 2020 clinical depression will become the second (second to chronic heart disease) international health disease burden, as measured by cause of death, disability, incapacity to work, and medical resources used. Moreover, major depression is a very costly disorder in terms of lost productivity at work, industrial accidents, bed occupancy in hospitals, treatment, state benefits, and personal sufferings (Gotlib & Hammen, 2002).

The illness also adversely affects interpersonal relationship with spouses and children (Gotlib & Hammen, 2002) and the rate of divorce is higher among depressives than among nondepressed individuals (Wade & Cairney, 2000), and the children of depressed parents are found to be at elevated risk of psychopathology (Gotlib & Goodman, 1999).

Approximately 60% of people who have a major depressive episode will have a second episode. Among those who have experienced two episodes, 70% will have a third, and among those who have had three episodes, 90% will have a fourth (APA, 2000). Depression also co-occurs with other disorders, both medical and psychiatric.

10.3 STAGES OF COGNITIVE HYPNOTHERAPY FOR DEPRESSION

Cognitive hypnotherapy generally consists of 16 weekly sessions, which can be expanded or modified according to the patient's clinical needs, areas of concern, and presenting symptoms. The stages of cognitive hypnotherapy are briefly described in this chapter. The sequence of the stages of treatment can be altered to suit the clinical needs of each patient.

10.4 SESSION 1: CLINICAL ASSESSMENT

Before initiating cognitive hypnotherapy, it is important for the therapist to take a detailed clinical history to formulate the diagnosis and identify the essential psychological, physiological, and social aspects of the patient's behaviors. This can be achieved by adopting a case-formulation approach to assessment (see Alladin, 2007, for a detailed description of case formulation with depression in the context of cognitive hypnotherapy).

10.5 SESSION 2: FIRST AID FOR DEPRESSION—PROTOCOL

As depressives tend to be plagued by feelings of low mood, hopelessness, and pessimism, any immediate relief from these feelings provides a sense of hope and optimism. Alladin (2006, 2007) and Overlade (1986) have described a First Aid technique for producing immediate relief from the pervasive depressed feeling. The First Aid technique consists of seven stages:

1. The patient is encouraged to talk about the situational factor that triggered or exacerbated the depressive affect and then allowed to ventilate feelings of distress and frustration.
2. A plausible biological explanation (natural adoption of a "tucking reflex" when hurt) of acute depression is provided to reduce guilt or self-blame for feeling depressed.
3. The hypnotic induction helps the patient to alter the depressive posture or "tucking response" by holding the head high and squaring the shoulders (advised to adopt the posture of a soldier on guard).

4. While in the hypnotic state, the patient is encouraged to make deliberate attempts to smile by imagining looking in a mirror.
5. Then the patient is encouraged to imagine a "funny face," while still experiencing hypnosis.
6. While in the state of hypnosis, the next step is to encourage the patient to "play a happy mental tape."
7. Finally, the patient learns to associate to a positive cue-word. The patient is given the posthypnotic suggestion that "From now on, whenever you feel down or depressed, and don't want to feel this way, all you have to do is to repeat the word *bubbles* and soon the bad feeling will ease away, replaced by good feeling."

10.6 SESSIONS 3–6: HYPNOTIC COGNITIVE BEHAVIOR THERAPY

At least four sessions are devoted to CBT, enhanced with hypnosis. The objects of the CBT sessions are to help the patients identify and restructure their dysfunctional beliefs that may be triggering and maintaining their depressive affect. Within the cognitive hypnotherapy framework, Alladin (2006, 2007) finds the following sequential presentation of the CBT components to be beneficial to the depressed patients.

The patient is offered a practical explanation of the cognitive model of depression and, as homework, the patient is advised to read the first three chapters from *Feeling Good: The New Mood Therapy* (Burns, 1999). The patient is encouraged to identify the cognitive distortions that form part of his or her negative rumination. The patient is advised to record them on the ABC Form (a form with three columns: A = Event; B = Automatic Thoughts; C = Emotional Responses). This homework helps the patient discover the link between thoughts (cognitions) and affect.

The concept of disputation or challenging of cognitive distortions is introduced after the patient had the opportunity to log the ABC Form for a week. The ABCDE Form permits the logging of disputation and the effects of disputation over negative affect. This form is an expanded version of the ABC Form, by including two extra columns (D = Disputation; E = Consequences of Disputation).

The patient is provided with a completed version of the ABCDE Form as an example of disputation. The patient is coached to differentiate between superficial ("I can't do this") and deeper ("I'm a failure") dysfunctional beliefs (negative self-schemas). The patient is coached on how to access and how to restructure deeper self-schemas. The patient is advised to constantly monitor and restructure negative cognitions until it becomes a habit.

10.7 SESSIONS 7–8: HYPNOSIS

Alladin (2006) and Yapko (1992) provide the following rationale for using hypnosis within the cognitive hypnotherapy framework. It induces relaxation, reduces distraction, maximizes concentration, facilitates divergent thinking, amplifies experiences, and provides access to nonconscious psychological processes.

The focus of the first two hypnotic sessions is on

1. Relaxation (to prove to the patient that he or she can relax)
2. Somatosensory changes (to reinforce the belief that the patient can have different feelings and sensations)
3. Demonstration of the power of the mind (via eye and body catalepsy)
4. Ego strengthening
5. Increasing confidence in the ability to utilize self-hypnosis

Here are some examples of the ego-strengthening suggestions adapted from Alladin (2006):

Day by day, as you listen to your self-hypnosis CD, you will become more relaxed, less anxious, and less depressed.

As a result of this treatment and as a result of you listening to your self-hypnosis CD every day, you will begin to feel more confident and you will begin to cope better with the changes and challenges of life every day.

You will begin to focus more and more on your achievements and successes than on your failures and shortcomings.

Posthypnotic suggestions (PHS) are also offered just before the end of the hypnosis session to counter negative self-hypnosis (NSH). Depressives tend to constantly ruminate with negative thoughts, feelings, and images (a form of NSH), especially following a stressful experience (e.g., "I will not be able to cope"). Here are some examples of PHS provided by Alladin (2006) for countering NSH:

While you are in an upsetting situation, you will become more aware of how to deal with it rather than focusing on your depressed feeling.

When you plan and take action to improve your future, you will feel more optimistic about the future.

As you get involved in doing things, you will be motivated to do more things.

At the end of the first hypnosis session, the patient is provided with a CD of self-hypnosis to induce relaxation, positive mental set, and a good frame of mind. The self-hypnosis CD also consists of ego-strengthening suggestions and posthypnotic suggestions. The homework assignment provides continuity of treatment between sessions and offers the patient the opportunity to learn self-hypnosis.

10.8 SESSIONS 9–12: COGNITIVE RESTRUCTURING USING HYPNOSIS

The next three sessions integrate the CBT and hypnotic strategies learned so far and also address nonconscious schemas. More specifically the sessions focus on (a) cognitive restructuring under hypnosis, (b) expansion of awareness and amplification of experiences, and (c) reduction of guilt and self-blame.

Hypnosis provides a powerful vehicle whereby cognitive distortions below the level of awareness can be explored and expanded. On occasions, in the course of CBT, the patient reports the inability to access cognitions preceding the depressive affect. As hypnosis provides access to unconscious cognitive distortions and negative self-schemas, unconscious maladaptive cognitions can be easily retrieved and restructured under hypnosis.

This is achieved by directing the patient's attention to the psychological contents of an experience or situation. The patient is guided to focus attention on a specific area of concern and establish the link between cognition and affect. Once the negative cognitions are identified, the patient is encouraged to restructure the maladaptive cognitions and then to attend to the resulting (desirable) responses.

For instance, if a person reports, "I don't know why I felt depressed at the party last week," the patient is hypnotically regressed back to the party and encouraged to identify and restructure the faulty cognitions associated with the party until the patient can think of the party without being upset.

10.9 OTHER HYPNOTIC OPPORTUNITIES

Hypnotic uncovering or restructuring procedures, such as affect bridge, age regression (Barabasz & Christensen, 2006; Christensen, Barabasz, & Barabasz, 2009), age progression, and dream induction can also be used to explore and restructure negative schemas (see Barabasz & Watkins, 2005; Daitch, 2007; Watkins & Barabasz, 2008).

Hypnosis provides a powerful device for expanding awareness and amplifying experience. Brown and Fromm (1990) describe a technique called enhancing affective experience and its expression for expanding and intensifying positive feelings. The object of this procedure is to help depressed patients create, amplify, and express a variety of negative and positive feelings and experience. The enhancing affective experience and its expression is specifically devised to (a) bring on underlying emotions into awareness, (b) create awareness of various feelings, (c) intensify positive affect, (d) enhance "discovered" affect, (e) induce positive moods, and (f) increase motivation. Such a technique not only disrupts the depressive cycle but also helps to develop antidepressive pathways.

10.10 SESSION 13: ATTENTION SWITCHING AND POSITIVE MOOD INDUCTION

Depressives have the tendency to become preoccupied with catastrophic thoughts and images. Such ruminations can easily become obsessional in nature and may kindle the brain to develop depressive pathways, thus impeding therapeutic progress. To counter the development of depressive pathways the positive mood induction technique is used.

Just as the brain can be kindled to produce depressive pathways through conscious negative focusing (Schwartz, Fair, Salt, Mandel, & Klerman, 1976), the brain can also be kindled to develop anti-depressive or happy pathways by focusing on positive imagery (Schwartz, 1984).

The positive mood induction technique consists of five steps: (1) education, (2) making a list of positive experiences, (3) positive mood induction, (4) posthypnotic suggestions, and (5) home practice. To educate the patient, the therapist provides a scientific rationale for producing antidepressive pathways. Then the patient is advised to make a list of 10 to 15 pleasant or positive experiences (e.g., a favorite holiday, a happy celebration, etc.). When in deep hypnosis, the patient is instructed to focus on a positive experience from the list of positive experiences, which is then amplified with assistance from the therapist. The technique is very similar to enhancing affective experience and its expression. However, to develop antidepressive pathways, more emphasis is placed on producing somatosensory changes to induce more pervasive concomitant physiological changes. While the patient is under hypnosis, the procedure is repeated with at least three positive experiences from the list of pleasant experiences.

Posthypnotic suggestions are provided so that the patient, with practice, will be able to become completely absorbed (regress) in the positive experience while practicing with the list at home.

10.11 SESSION 14: ACTIVE INTERACTIVE TRAINING

The active interactive training technique helps to break "dissociative" habits and encourages "association" with the pertinent environment. When interacting with their internal or external environment, depressives tend to reflexively dissociate to negative schemas rather than actively interact with the pertinent external information.

Active interaction means being alert and in tune with the incoming information (conceptual reality), whereas reflexive dissociation is the tendency to anchor or submit to "inner reality" (negative schemas and associated syncretic feelings), which inhibits reality testing or appraisal of conceptual reality.

To prevent reflexive dissociation a person (a) must become aware of the automatic occurrence of such a process, (b) actively attempt to inhibit it by switching attention away from "bad anchors," and (c) actively attend to pertinent cues or conceptual reality.

10.12 SESSION 15: SOCIAL SKILLS TRAINING

There is evidence (Youngren & Lewinshon, 1980) that lack of social skills may cause and maintain depression in some patients. A session (or more sessions as required) is therefore devoted to teaching social skills. The social skills training can be enhanced by hypnosis via imagery training, imaginal rehearsal, ego strengthening, and posthypnotic suggestions.

10.13 SESSION 16: IDEAL GOALS/REALITY TRAINING AND CONCLUSIONS

While under hypnosis, the patient is encouraged to imagine ideal but realistic goals, and then to imagine planning appropriate strategies and taking necessary actions for achieving them (forward projection with behavioral rehearsal).

10.14 BOOSTER AND FOLLOW-UP SESSIONS

Hypnosis, as outlined in this chapter, normally requires 16 weekly individual sessions. Some depressed patients may, however, require fewer or more sessions. After these sessions, further booster or follow-up sessions may be provided as required.

10.15 CONCLUSIONS

MDD is among one of the most common psychiatric disorders treated by psychiatrists and psychotherapists. Although MDD can sometimes be treated successfully with costly antidepressant medication and psychotherapy, a significant number of depressives do not respond to these approaches. Cognitive hypnotherapy, a multimodal treatment, is cost effective and can be made available to a wide range of patients with MDD, with validated benefits.

Chapter 11

Stress and anxiety

Stephen Kahn

> People do not think their way into new ways of acting, they
> always act their way into new ways of thinking.

> —**Erich Fromm**

11.1 INTRODUCTION

Woven throughout most treatment modalities and in both psychological and medical procedures is the treatment of anxiety. The
most common disorders of anxiety are phobias, including agoraphobia, and generalized anxiety disorder. More serious anxiety
disorders such as posttraumatic stress disorder (see Chapter 6) or
obsessive–compulsive disorder involve more complicated treatments and follow-ups.

11.2 RESEARCH

Research on the efficacy of hypnosis with anxiety is clearly evidenced
in many treatment protocols, which have been published utilizing
controlled studies to test efficacy (O'Neill, Barnier, & McConkey,
1999; Sapp, 1992). Using hypnosis enhances the cognitive component used to manage anxiety and stress (Kirsch, Montgomery,
& Sapirstein, 1995; Schoenberger, 1996) and for public speaking
anxiety (Schoenberger, Kirsch, Gearan, Montgomery, & Pastyrnak,
1997). It has been proven effective in treating panic disorder with
agoraphobia (Starfrace, 1994). It reduces anxiety and enhances
well-being in pain/burn (Frenay, Faymonville, Devlieger, Albert,

& Vanderkelen, 2001; also see Chapters 3 and 4 on pain in this volume) and medical patients (Gruzelier et al., 2002; Kiecolt-Glaser, Marucha, Atkinson, & Glaser, 2001; Lang, Joyce, Spiegel, Hamilton, & Lee, 1996; Lu & Lu, 1996). Hypnosis has been proven effective with test anxiety as well (Sapp, 1991; Stanton, 1994) and with coping with school stress in students (Whitehouse et al., 1996).

II.3 ASSESSMENT

The assessment phase of treatment for stress and anxiety includes a thorough history that assesses not just changes in the symptoms over time, but includes symptom coping strategies, associated stresses, and impact on lifestyle. In addition, the patient's strengths, including both cognitive and emotional resources as well as methods of self-soothing and relaxation, are indicated. This is usually completed by the end of the first session. The homework assignment is self-monitoring of the symptoms on an hourly basis, including what influences their appearance and disappearance have on any associated stresses. Daily comments on this process illuminate possibly unconsidered factors and help facilitate new insight.

Many patients with generalized anxiety disorder ascertain triggers they did not realize were affecting them. High-risk times and situations become apparent and can be utilized in the stages of treatment. In addition, factors that decrease anxiety become clearer. Just using self-monitoring itself helps decrease anxiety.

II.4 FOUR STAGES OF TREATMENT OF ANXIETY

The specific treatment of anxiety involves four stages with each resting on the earlier stage. Lynn and Kirsch (2006) propose a similar set of evidenced-based treatments for anxiety. The first stage aims at visceral control. Once this has been achieved and the patient can relax at will quickly and easily, the patient can begin to work on desensitization. Once the patient can readily relax in or near anxiety-evoking situations or whenever the anxiety strikes, the cognitive work can begin. Finally, rehearsal strategies are employed in which all previous strategies are utilized.

1. Visceral control—Relaxation therapies are used in virtually all anxiety therapies (Barlow, 2002). Thus, therapy begins with using hypnosis and self-hypnosis to teach the patient to relax in nonstressful circumstances. Usually in the second session hypnosis for relaxation, focusing on breathing and on muscle relaxation and other soothing images, is performed. Posthypnotic suggestions for quicker and easier achievement of deeper relaxation can be given. If the patient can achieve a reasonable depth of trance and relaxation, then a recording (cassette or CD) can be created for him or her to practice at home, usually twice a day. This should be at a time when the patient is already somewhat relaxed and removed from either internal or external distractions.

   A patient who is unable to achieve a relaxed state in the office should not be pushed into it. After trying a number of different types of inductions, the therapist can discuss resistance or even use paradox or other indirect methods a la Erickson (Erickson & Rossi, 1979) to get the patient to relax. Once this is achieved, only then should the patient attempt self-hypnosis (Fromm & Kahn, 1990).

   Eventual mastery of this stage is evidenced by the patient's ability to go to a deep level of relaxation in just a few minutes and in most everyday situations. Usually a verbal or visual or bodily cue (hand on chest and say to yourself "relax") is utilized.

2. Desensitization—Exposure therapies have a long history of proven effectiveness in treating anxiety (Barlow, 2002). Hypnosis enhances this work. Typically, the patient creates a hierarchy of feared situations or objects. Graded exposure (starting with the least feared circumstance) in hypnosis allows the patient to experientially process his reactions and learn to modulate them by inducing the relaxation response in the imagined presence of anxiety-producing situations. A television screen can give more distance and put the control (remote control) in the patient's hands, where the patient can shift from the anxiety situation to the "relaxation channel."

3. Cognitive—Interventions can be introduced after desensitization has been achieved. Hypnosis enhances this cognitive work (Kirsch et al., 1995). Cognitions, particularly catastrophizing and generalization, can be rewritten since the anxiety

can be countered with the thought "I have mastered my fear and feel confident I can manage my anxiety." The patient can now confidently state that the anxiety is under his control.

4. Rehearsal—This is the final stage in which the patient in hypnosis goes through the entire scene, utilizing his new coping strategies to relieve his stress and anxiety. Once this has been mastered in imagination, that is, little or no anxiety throughout the whole stressful situation, the patient is ready for controlled rehearsal in vivo (Barlow, 2002). For instance, if the patient is suffering from a flying phobia, he can simulate his trip to the airport, approaching the gate and even waiting in line to board, before he actually attempts the flight.

11.5 CONCLUSIONS

Hypnosis is an effective and powerful intervention for most types of stress and anxiety. With more severe anxiety disorders, such as obsessive–compulsive disorder and posttraumatic stress disorder, intervention is much more complex and varied. Administering anxiety treatment with a stage-specific methodology can effectively manage panic disorder and agoraphobia, generalized anxiety disorder, phobias, and social anxiety disorder.

Chapter 12

Procedural hypnosis

Elvira V. Lang

12.1 DEVELOPMENT OF PROCEDURAL HYPNOSIS

Procedural hypnosis is defined as a hypnotic intervention provided for a patient who undergoes surgery, medical procedures of any kind, imaging or invasive tests, or is distressed by a medical office visit. Procedural hypnosis can be applied as a stand-alone means of managing pain and anxiety, or can be used as an adjunct to local anesthesia, oral or intravenous drugs, and even general anesthesia. In my experience, procedural hypnosis consists of 70% advanced rapport skills, which validate the patient, and 30% specific hypnotic skills (Lang et al., 1999). A trained member of the procedure team can successfully apply procedural hypnosis by reading a hypnosis script, which takes about 5 minutes.

The choice to use procedural hypnosis is often born out of necessity. In 1845 Esdaile, a Scottish surgeon working in India, became so distraught by the screaming and sufferance of a patient during a surgery that he decided to use "mesmerism" for the next procedure. It worked and the experience propelled Esdaile to become a pioneer in the use of hypnosis as anesthesia for surgery (Esdaile, 1846). He built a distinguished career on this concept and even had a mesmeric hospital in Calcutta dedicated to this practice. Esdaile achieved not only pain reduction, but also observed a reduced rate of infections and had no patients die from surgery—quite a competitive advantage. However, the discovery of ether and, shortly thereafter, chloroform shifted enthusiasm of the clinical establishment toward pharmaceutical options of anesthesia and largely away from the benefits of procedural hypnosis.

Esdaile's push toward hypnosis out of necessity likely repeats itself many times all over the world, as long as there is an individual present who has been trained in hypnosis and dares to step forward. I first witnessed hypnosis when I had to perform a relatively minor procedure on a young Vietnam War veteran about 18 years ago. He was horribly frightened to just even lie on the procedure table and receive local anesthetic. One of the technologists asked to use an imagery process, and upon seeing the success I decided to dedicate my future research to the topic of procedural hypnosis. Introducing hypnosis in a surgery suite, delivery ward, or in the dentist office requires some effort and guts if the environment is hypnosis naive or even hypnosis averse. Such efforts were hampered in the past by the lack of published validation. By now, however, there is enough evidence showing that procedural hypnosis reduces pain, anxiety, complications, and cost.

The major international professional hypnosis societies—the Society for Clinical and Experimental Hypnosis (SCEH) and the International Society of Hypnosis (ISH)—long believed that the training and practice of hypnosis should be reserved for mental health care professionals, physicians, dentists, and social workers with some extension to master-level nurses. Hypnosis was considered a time-intensive and deep-reaching effort—just as Esdaile in the beginning performed a rather extensive and exhausting mesmeric act. Large-scale studies, however, have shown that a relatively quick hypnotic induction on the operating table can have excellent results (Lang et al., 1996, 2000, 2006). This opened the path to include the healthcare professionals who are at the front line of treating patient distress. The New England Society of Clinical Hypnosis in the United States was the first to include registered nurses and technologists in its membership and training criteria, a move followed by SCEH in 2008. Licensed health care professionals will, from now on, be officially allowed to provide patients procedural hypnosis within the realm of their usual duties. It is believed that this will help spread the practice and hopefully provide any patient who can benefit from it the advantages of procedural hypnosis. Having a low-risk adjunct or alternative to pharmacological sedation has the potential to prevent 26,000 deaths and serious complications annually in United States alone that could be expected based on the rate of procedures performed under conscious sedation. On a worldwide basis, the potential numbers could easily exceed 100,000 per year.

12.2 EVIDENCE FOR THE EFFICACY OF PROCEDURAL HYPNOSIS

Past trials showed that patients' pain perception during invasive medical procedures increases over time regardless of the amount of drugs administered (Lang et al., 2000, 2006, 2008). Large-scale prospective randomized studies of patients undergoing vascular and renal procedures, large-core breast biopsy, and percutaneous tumor treatment demonstrated that a short hypnosis on the procedure table interrupts this pattern and significantly reduces the pain and anxiety (Lang et al., 2000, 2006, 2008). In addition, patients use lower dosages and fewer drugs, or none at all, and have significantly fewer complications. Brief hypnosis prior to surgical removal of breast lumps also has been reported to reduce pain, nausea, fatigue, discomfort, and emotional upset as compared to controls (Montgomery et al., 2007). Improved patient outcomes with periprocedural hypnosis have also been documented in a variety of other settings including burn care; plastic surgery; labor and delivery; the removal of appendices, bone marrow, teeth, and tonsils; and first-trimester pregnancy termination (Butler, Symons, Henderson, Shortliffe, & Spiegel, 2005; Faymonville, Meurisse, & Fissette, 1999; Marc et al., 2008; Patterson, Everett, Burns, & Marvin, 1992; Wain, 2004; Zeltzer & LeBaron, 1982).

Fortunately procedural hypnosis is resource sensitive. If hypnosis were provided to all patients having surgical lumpectomy, $772.71 could be saved per case (Montgomery et al., 2007). If it were applied to all patients undergoing outpatient vascular procedures, an average of $330 could be saved per case (Lang & Rosen, 2002). These savings are largely due to prevention of oversedation occurring with pharmacologic anesthesia and are realized even if the person structuring hypnosis is added to the team and paid extra.

12.3 CONSIDERATIONS

The doctor's office, hospital, and surgery suite are environments that produce a high level of hypnotic responsiveness. Patients listen carefully to every word that is said. This makes procedural hypnosis relatively easy to administer, if done correctly, but also bears risks when well-meaning health professionals unknowingly induce harm by giving inappropriate suggestions, as is sometimes the case in nonhypnotic interventions, such as distraction. Wording with negative conations such as *burn, pain,* and *sting* increase patients' pain and anxiety, even when they are qualified by *little* or *no* (Lang et al., 2005). A recent trial with patients who underwent invasive tumor treatment had to be halted when patients in the empathic attention control group had a very high adverse event rate (Lang et al., 2008). This was mainly due to personnel in the room—other than the person displaying structured empathic attention skills—all wanting to be especially nice to the patients and chiming in, thereby likely producing continued sympathetic arousal. When patients during this trial had a hypnosis script read, the entire atmosphere in the room was quieter and procedural progress was much smoother, more rapid, and less dramatic. This experience showed how important it is to give medical personnel the means to express their empathy in a way that helps the patient and also helps the personnel to overcome their own anxiety. Procedural hypnosis offers just such a solution. It takes a village where all have an understanding about the hypnotic process even if not all team members actively practice it. This will reduce the risk of sabotage and enable the communication training that health care professionals may otherwise reject as unnecessary in consideration of their perceived excellent skills. Therefore, team training on site is viewed as the best way to achieve the operating room of the future where "high tech" and "high touch" go hand in hand.

12.4 CONCLUSIONS

Procedural hypnosis is an effective and resource-sensitive approach to providing patients and health care professionals less stress and better outcomes. Its practice does not require any props and can be performed under the most and also the least sophisticated environments, requiring only a willing and trained hypnosis practitioner.

Appendix A: Hypnosis glossary

abreaction: A physical movement or an emotional outburst as a reaction to a suggestion while in the state of hypnosis. Hypnotic abreaction is one technique often employed in ego state therapy and various forms of hypnoanalysis to release repressed material and facilitate personality reconstruction (e.g., posttraumatic stress disorder). A panic attack or flashback can also be thought of as an abreaction. They can occur outside of therapy and can be initiated by a variety of things (i.e., misinterpretation of a situation or someone's words/actions) and are commonly unrelated to the source of the original trauma. When trauma is resolved, no further abreactions associated with that trauma will occur, as is the goal of ego state therapy and hypnoanalysis for PTSD and ASD.

affect bridge: A technique used to discover the origin of a neurotic symptom to facilitate the process of resolution. Hypnosis is used to evoke unwanted symptomatized emotions, followed by questions concerning those feelings, and a request to return (via hypnotic age regression) to a previous time when those feelings were experienced.

affirmations: Positive suggestions given in hypnosis. Affirmations are a useful method of enhancing a patient's self-esteem and can serve to facilitate activation of inner strength.

age regression: Refers to a hypnotized participant who is given suggestions of a return to a younger age so that certain experiences are reactivated and re-experienced. The goal is the resolution of emotional trauma or relief of pain. Age regression is topographical rather than temporal. Thus, the "revivication" is the primary process with the associated affect from an earlier part of one's life rather than a literal going back in time.

alpha state: A state of relaxed wakefulness achieved by individuals who produce a predominance of alpha wave EEG activity. It may occur or be increased as a result of biofeedback, meditation, yoga, hypnosis, and other calmly focused activities (contrary to common belief, the presence of alpha 7½ to 13½ Hz is not a specific marker of the hypnotic state).

altered state of consciousness (ASC): A state of psychological functioning that is significantly different from ordinary states of consciousness. ASCs are characterized by altered levels of self-awareness, affect, reality testing, orientation to time and place, wakefulness, responsiveness to external stimuli, a sense of ecstasy, boundlessness, or "unity with the universe." Superficial ASCs such as being engrossed in reading a book, watching a movie, and lack of awareness due to repetitive, monotonous activity are typically accompanied by disturbed temporal sense, constriction of perception, or a feeling of deep pleasurable involvement. More profound ASCs such as in hypnosis, sensory deprivation (SD), restricted environmental stimulation (REST), or some drug-induced states have been reported as the experience of mystical feelings, such as partaking in universal oneness, or enhanced or complete understanding. Although psychoanalysis has tended to regard them as regressive phenomena, other contexts, such as in certain Eastern philosophies and transpersonal psychology, regard them as higher states of consciousness and often indicative of a more profound level of personal and spiritual evolution.

alter: Commonly used to describe a personality state of a person with dissociative identity disorder (DID). An alter is typically not consciously aware of other alters present in the same patient. Alters contrast with the surface states of nonpathological individuals where intercommunication works well with hypnosis.

anchor: A specific stimulus such as a word, image, or touch that through the rule of association evokes a particular mental, emotional, and physiological state.

awakening: An act of bringing a person out of trance and into full (waking) conscious awareness.

body syndrome: A physical manifestation of an emotional trauma, which is held in or repressed instead of being processed and released. Certain body parts may be more inclined to harbor these manifestations depending on individual's idiosyncratic experiences.

congruence: Occurs when goals, thoughts, and behaviors are in agreement.

conscience: The ability to judge correctly on moral issues. The super ego as conceived in psychoanalysis, hypnoanalysis, and ego state therapy is viewed as functioning in substantively the same way as conscience. Thus, there is a more or less integrated functioning of a person's system of moral values in approval or disapproval of one's own acts or proposed acts. Alternative ego states may vary in super ego functions.

conscious mind: The ability to react to the environment by having sensations, feelings, thoughts, and strivings; being aware.

deepening techniques/hypnotic depth: The required depth of hypnosis is dependent on the demands of the specific procedure. Little hypnotic depth is required to reduce anxiety by activating relaxation/calmness in contrast to the level of hypnotic involvement essential to painless surgery without an anesthetic. Depth adequate to achieve the suggested response may not be automatically manifested upon exposure to a hypnotic induction (Kahn & Fromm, 2001). (See Barabasz & Watkins, 2005, pp. 186–201, for deepening protocols, e.g., fractionation, summer day, progressive warmth, descending stairs, timed breathing, floating in a cloud, revolving wheels, etc.)

defense mechanism: An unconscious reaction pattern employed by the ego to protect itself from anxiety that arises from intrapsychic conflict. Such mechanisms range from the mature to immature depending on how much they distort reality. They operate on an unconscious level and they serve to deny or distort reality, thoughts, and action. Some defense mechanisms are repression, denial, rationalization, projection, displacement, turning against self, reaction formation, overcompensation, intellectualization, withdrawal, regression, and sublimation. Denial, displacement, and projection are immature (maladaptive), whereas sublimation is most mature because it allows (an adaptive/productive) indirect satisfaction of a true wish.

direct hypnotic suggestion: Takes the form of a command or specific instruction after evocation of the hypnotic state.

dissociation: Can involve hypnotically induced anesthesia or sedation. There is no loss of consciousness. It may involve a picture or visual image where the patient visually observes his or her body from the outside. It has been described as seeing life from the perspective of a camera or floating above oneself.

ecology: Derived from the biological sciences; concerns the whole person/organization as a balanced, interacting system. When a change is ecological, the whole person and organization (or family) benefits.

ego state: An integrated state of mind that determines the individual's relationships to the environment and to other people. Each is distinguished by a particular role, mood, and mental function, which when executive assumes first person identity. Ego states are normal parts of a healthy psyche and should not be confused with alters (multiple personalities) that are manifested and shown in people with dissociative identity disorder.

executive: An ego state or alter is executive when conscious and able to communicate or function external to the individual. Some nonexecutive ego states can hear a conversation, whereas others will not. Only one state is executive at a given time, but states may switch the executive rapidly.

eye fixation induction: Typically involves asking the patient to focus. The patient is asked to stare at an object above eye level. The practitioner might tell the patient that his eyelids are getting heavier and beginning to close. (See Barabasz & Watkins, 2005, for protocols.)

fight or flight: A primitive and involuntary reaction that is triggered during danger or anxiety to protect oneself or to escape from danger.

glove anesthesia: A type of hypnoanesthesia when the patient's hand is made to feel numb, and the numbness can be transferred to the part of the body required by the procedure. This is a direct hypnotic suggestion in contrast to one involving a more abstract form of dissociation.

guided imagery (guided affective imagery):   The drawing out of emotional fantasies to ease catharsis and confront emotions that would otherwise be painful to the patient. The practitioner suggests images that would bring up emotional states, images of physical relaxation, or images of a desired future success. The procedure can induce hypnosis in a responsive patient. It involves the focused use of imagination (not fantasy).

hypnosis: See Chapter 1.

hypnotic susceptibility: See **hypnotizability.**

hypnotizability: The current descriptor of a person's ability to respond to hypnosis. It is not related to gender, IQ, or non-hypnotic suggestibility. Hypnotizability was introduced by Ernest R. Hilgard (1979) to replace the outdated term *hypnotic susceptibility.* Hypnotizability is now the preferred term by most of the published leaders in the field (Christensen, 2005).

ideomotor response/automatic finger signal: Automatic finger signaling is a finger movement in response to a question, such as if you can hear me, move a finger or if it's OK to go deeper into hypnosis move a finger.

induction: See Chapter 1.

initial sensitizing event: An emotional event that is thought to be the origin of a specific problem. For example, claustrophobia could be traced back to being locked in a closet in early childhood.

introject: An internal manifestation of a person significant in one's life. (See Watkins & Barabasz, 2008.)

malevolent ego state: A state that appears to purposely act inappropriately to either other ego states of the person or to the outside world. Malevolent ego states were originally manifested to protect the person early in life. Via ego state therapy, they can assume a positive function.

mapping ego states: Use of hypnosis to learn about the presence and nature of a person's particular ego states. The process includes learning the internal relationships of the states. After mapping, the patient will have a better self-understanding and can learn to call forward the executive or a preferred state for a particular situation (see Emmerson, 2003).

mesmerism: An early term for hypnosis named after Franz Anton Mesmer.

mirroring: Putting oneself in the same posture as another person in an effort to establish or enhance rapport.

parataxic distortion: Occurs when one responds to a person or situation in a distorted way. The patient is not responding to the situation or person but rather to what is subconsciously triggered.

paris window: Used to widen the perspective of patients so they can see their problems from more than their own viewpoint. The window has four panes. Three panes contain a question for the client: (1) How do you feel about the problem? (2) How do you think others feel about your problem? (3) How do you feel about how others feel about your problem? The fourth pane is thought to shed light on the answer to the patient's problem based on this newfound perspective. When hypnosis is used adjunctively to a psychotherapeutic technique, it serves to facilitate progress and reduce defensive reactions. Conscious defenses are usually less problematic when the patient is experiencing hypnosis.

parts therapy: A complex hypnotic technique where the therapist talks with various constructed parts of the mind. The "inner child" and "inner adult" is viewed by some as part of ego state therapy.

primary process: A psychoanalytic term referring to the id process by which there is immediate and direct satisfaction of an instinctual wish or that aspect of conscious activity that represents it. It does not discriminate between image and reality, hence, in the absence of an immediately satisfying object or situation, an imagery satisfaction is produced. The laws governing primary process are different from those of consciousness. Age regression, by hypnosis, activates primary process for therapeutic purposes such as in trauma resolution.

secondary gain: A reason, primarily subconscious, why a person continues to perform a certain behavior.

secondary process: Conscious activity involving action guided by essentially objective realities. Such activity in psychoanalytic terms is in the preconscious or ego.

sequential progressive relaxation: A type of induction involving the progressive relaxation of various parts of the body. (See Barabasz & Watkins, 2005, for protocols.)

stage hypnosis: The public use of social influence and waking suggestion for entertainment purposes. It may or may not involve genuine hypnosis.

stages of loss: There are five stages a person goes through to deal with a loss. Not every individual will display all the symptoms nor in the same time or manner. The stages are (1) denial, (2) anger, (3) bargaining, (4) grief, and (5) resolution.

surface states: An Ego State Therapy term referring to those states that are most often executive for normal daily function. They have good communication among one another. Thus, they are cognitive and deliberative. Clinically, surface states may be accessed with or without hypnosis.

switching: Occurs when a state is executive and a different ego state becomes executive.

sympathetic–parasympathetic: The two divisions of the autonomic nervous system. When activated, the sympathetic system causes physiological changes to occur, preparing the body for fight or flight. The parasympathetic system is self-regulating and stabilizing. It serves to bring a person back to a state of balance or homeostasis.

time distortion: A phenomenon where one loses conscious awareness of how much time has passed (5 minutes can seem like 20 minutes or vice versa). Time distortion is common in hypnosis whether suggested or not. It is often specifically suggested to promote relief of pain or hypnotically minimize a patient's perception of the duration of a painful medical procedure or for childbirth. (See McCarthy, 2001.)

underlying states: States that only rarely become executive. They have little communication with surface states. These states are essentially inaccessible without hypnosis. They contain positive and pleasant memories as well as unresolved trauma. For example, a person who sees a type of wallpaper or smells a particular odor like that of a childhood room may experience an underlying ego state, bringing about childhood feelings and vivid memories. Some of these memories may have been unknown to the surface states. Ego state therapy provides specific techniques for accessing such states to effect a corrective restructuring of the personality. (See Watkins & Barabasz, 2008.)

Appendix B: Contributor contacts

Chapter 1 Hypnotic Concepts (Barabasz and Christensen)
arreedbarabasz@wsu.com
ijceh@pullman.com

Chapter 2 Hypnosis Testing (Spiegel)
dspiegel@stanford.edu

Chapter 3 Acute Pain (Patterson)
davepatt@u.washington.edu

Chapter 4 Chronic Pain (Jensen)
mjensen@u.washington.edu

Chapter 5 Childhood Problems (Olness and Kohen)
karen.olness@casse.edu
dpkohen@umn.edu

Chapter 6 Posttraumatic Stress Disorder (PTSD) (Vermetten and Christensen)
E.Vermetten@umcutrecht.nl
ijceh@pullman.com

Chapter 7 Surgery (Thomson)
Linda.M.R.Thomson@Hitchcock.org

Chapter 8 Childbirth (Irland)
jmirland@hotmail.com

Chapter 9 Hypnosis and Sleep (Yapko)
michaelyapko@roadrunner.com

Chapter 10 Depression (Alladin)
assen.alladin@calgaryhealthregion.ca

Chapter 11 Stress and Anxiety (Kahn)
spkahn@ameritech.net

Chapter 12 Procedural Hypnosis (Lang)
elang@bidmc.harvard.edu

Appendix C: International and national societies of hypnosis

INTERNATIONAL SOCIETIES OF HYPNOSIS

Society for Clinical and Experimental Hypnosis (SCEH)
Massachusetts School of Professional Psychology
221 Rivermoor Street
Boston, MA 02132
Phone: (617) 469-1981
Toll free number: (888) 664-6777, ext. 203
Fax: (617) 469-1889
E-mail: sceh@mspp.edu
Web site: www.sceh.us or http://educ.wsu.edu
Publication: *International Journal of Clinical and Experimental Hypnosis (IJCEH)*. The major citation impact journal in the field.
Editor: Prof. Arreed Franz Barabasz, EdD, PhD, ABPP
Washington State University
P.O. Box 642136
Pullman, WA 99164-2136
Phone: (509) 335-8166
E-mail: ijceh@pullman.com
Web site: http://www.ijceh.com

International Society of Hypnosis (ISH)
Austin & Repatriation Medical Centre
Repatriation Campus, 300 Waterdale Road
Heidelberg Heights VIC 3081
Australia
Phone: +61 3 9496 4105
Fax: +61 3 9496 4107

E-mail: ish-central.office@medicine.unimelb.edu.au
Web site: http://www.ish.unimelb.edu.au/ish.html
Publication: *International Journal of Clinical and Experimental Hypnosis*

NATIONAL SOCIETIES OF HYPNOSIS

American Psychological Association Division 30—The Society of Psychological Hypnosis
750 First Street, NE
Washington, DC 20002-4242
Phone: (800) 374-2721, (202) 336-5500, (202) 336-6013
TDD: (202) 336-6123
Fax: (202) 218-3599
Publications: *International Journal of Clinical and Experimental Hypnosis*; *Psychological Hypnosis* (quarterly newsletter)

American Society of Clinical Hypnosis (ASCH)
140 N. Bloomingdale Rd.
Bloomingdale, IL 60108-1017
Phone: (630) 980-4740
Fax: (630) 351-8490
E-mail: info@asch.net
Web site: http://www.asch.net
Publications: *American Journal of Clinical Hypnosis* (AJCH), Editor: Thurman Mott, MD; *Newsletter of the American Society of Clinical Hypnosis* (quarterly)

Association Francaise d'Hypnotherapi
74, Rue Lamarck
75018 Paris
France
E-mail: dfayolet@noos.fr
Web site: www.afhyp.org

Associazionne Medica Italiana per lo Studio dell Ipnosi (AMISI)
E-mail: amisi@mw.itline.it

Australian Society of Hypnosis (ASH)
Victoria Branch, ASH

P.O. Box 5114
Alphington VIC 3078
Australia
Phone: +61 3 9458 5133
Fax: +61 3 9458 5399
E-mail: hypnosis@alphalink.com.au
Publication: *Australian Journal of Clinical and Experimental Hypnosis* (AJCEH)
  P.O. Box 592
  Heidelberg VIC 3084
  Australia
  Phone: +61 3 9496 4621
  Fax: +61 3 9496 4564
  E-mail: bevans@alphalink,com.au
  Web site: http://www.ozhypnosis.com.au/publications.htm

British Association of Medical Hypnosis (BAMH)
  15 Connaught Square
  London W2 2HG
  United Kingdom
  Phone: +44 0171- 706 7775
  Fax: +44 0171- 262 1237
  E-mail: secretary@bamh.org.uk
  Web site: http://www.bamh.org.uk/

British Society of Experimental and Clinical Hypnosis (BSECH)
  Hollybank House, Lees Road
  Mossley, Ashton-u-Lyne
  OL5 OPL
  United Kingdom
  Phone/Fax: 01457 839363
  E-mail: honsec@bsech.com
  Web site: http://www.bsech.com
  Publication: *Contemporary Hypnosis*
    Editor: John Gruzelier
    Blackhorse Road
    Letchworth
    Herts SG6 1HN
    Phone: 01462 672555
    Fax: 01462 480947

British Society of Medical and Dental Hypnosis (BSMDH)
28 Dale Park Gardens
Cookridge, Leeds
LS16 7PT
United Kingdom
Phone/Fax: 07000 560309
E-mail: Nat.office@bsmdh.org
Website: http://www.bsmdh.org

Centor Ericksoniano de Mexico (CEM)
E-mail: erickmex@hipnosis.com.mx
Web site: www.hipnosis.com.mx

Centro Italiano Ipnosi Clinico-Sperimentale (CIICS)
E-mail: ciis@seleneweb.com

Centro Studi de Ipnosi Clinica e Psiocoterapia "H. Bernheim"
(CSICHB) (Italy)
E-mail: dirsan@villarosa.it

Danish Society of Clinical Hypnosis (DSH)
Web site: http://www.hypnoterapi.com

Dansk Selskab for Klinisk Hypnose (DSKH)
Rosenborggade 12
1130 Copenhagen K
Denmark
E-mail: hypnosis@get2net.dk

Deutshe Gesellschaft fur arztliche Hypnose und Autogenes
Training E.V. (DGAHAT)
Sekretariat
Postfach 1365
41463 Neuss
Germany
Web site: http://www.dgaehat.de

Deutshe Gesellschaft fur zahnarztliche Hypnose (DGZH)
Esslinger Strasse 40
70182 Stuttgart
Germany
E-mail: mail@dgzh.de
Web site: http://www.dgzh.de

Dutch Society of Hypnosis (Nvvh—Nederlands vereniging voor hypnose)
Nvvh, Herenstraat 1-B
3512KA Utrecht
The Netherlands
E-mail: secretariat@nvvh.com or info@nvvh.com
Web site: http://www.nvvh.com
Publication: *International Journal of Clinical and Experimental Hypnosis* (see information for Society for Clinical and Experimental Hypnosis for details)

European Society of Hypnosis (ESH)
ESH Central Office
Inspiration House
Redbrook Grove
Sheffield
S20 6RR
United Kingdom
Web site: http://www.esh-hypnosis.eu
E-mail: mail@esh-hypnosis.eu

Flemish Society of Hypnosis (VHYP—Vlaams Wetenschappelijke Hypnose Vereniging)
Honingstraat 5 2220 Heist-op-den-Berg
Phone/Fax: 015 245183
E-mail: vhyp@village.uunet.be
Web site: http://www.vhyp.be

German Society of Hypnosis (DGH)
Druffelsweg 3
48653 Coesfeld
Germany
E-mail: DGH-Geschaeftsstelle@t-online.de
Publication: *Experimentelle und Klinische Hypnose*

New Zealand Society of Hypnosis (NZSH)
Wellington, New Zealand
Phone: 04 385 6998
E-mail: cmc89@telstra.net.nz
Web site: http://www.nzsh.org.nz/

Hungarian Association of Hypnosis (HAH)
E-mail: mhesecretary@hotmail.com or GGACS@IZABELL.
ELTE.hu

Indian Society of Clinical and Experimental Hypnosis (ISCEH)
E-mail: mrs_shovajana@im.eth.net

Israel Society of Hypnosis (IsSH)
E-mail: ewa@netvision.net.il
Web site: http://www.hypno.co.il or http://www.hypno.org.il

Japan Society of Hypnosis (JSH)
E-mail: jsh@human.tsukuba.ac.jp

MEG, Milton H. Erickson Gesellschaft für Klinische Hypnose
e.V.
Waisenhausstrasse 55
80637 Munich
Germany
E-mail: monika-kohl@t-online.de
Web sites: http://www.milton-erickson-gesellschaft.de or http://
www.MEG-hypnose.de
Publication: *Hypnose und Kognition*

Mexican Society of Hypnosis (MSH)
E-mail: Erickson@iwm.com.mx

Norwegian Society for Clinical and Experimental Hypnosis
(NFKEH—Norsk Forening for Klinisk og Ekspeimentell
Hypnose)
E-mail: guro@smerteklinikken.com
Web site: www.hypnoseforeningen.no

Osterreichische Gesellschaft fur Autogens Training und
Allgenmeine Psychotherapie (OGATAP)
OGATAP Secretariat
Kaiser str. 14/13
1070 Vienna
Austria
E-mail: office@oegatap.at

Sociedade Brasileira de Hipnose
  Rua Jacirendi, 60
  CEP 030066-00 Tatuape
  Sao Paulo, Brazil
  E-mail: joelpriori@starmedia.com
  Web site: www.sbhh.org.br/

Societa Italiana di Ipnosi (SII)
  E-mail: ipnosii@tin.it
  Web site: http://www.hypnosis.it

Societe Quebecoise d'Hypnose Inc. (SQH)
  Bureau 485
  1575 Boul. Henri-Bourassa oust
  Montreal, Quebec H3M 3A9
  Canada
  E-mail: cpgb@qc.aira.com

South African Society of Clinical Hypnosis (SASCH)
  E-mail: sasch@cis.co.za

Swedish Society of Clinical and Experimental Hypnosis (SSCEH)
  SFKH's kansli, Flat 3, S-931 85 Skelleftea
  E-mail: ssceh@telia.com
  Web site: http://www.hypnos-se.org
  Publication: *Hypnos*

Swiss Medical Society of Hypnosis (SMSH)
  E-mail: smsh@smile.ch
  Web site: http://www.smsh.ch

Swiss Society for Clinical Hypnosis (SHypS)
  E-mail: peter.hin@bluewin.ch
  Web site: http://www.hypnos.ch

Tieteellinen Hypnoosi—Vetenskaplig Hypnose (TH-VH)
  Kylatie8 M 6
  16300 Ormattila
  Finland
  E-mail: timo.heinonen@pp2.inet.fi
  Web site: http://www.hypnoosi.net

Vlaamse Wetenschappelijke Hypnose Vereniging
  517 3070 Kortenberg
  Belgium
  E-mail: vhyp@village.uunet.be
  Web site: http://www.vhyp.be

Appendix D: Further study

Barabasz A., & Christensen, C. (2009). Hypnosis induction demonstrations: Techniques, metaphors, and scripts. DVD.

Barabasz A., & Watkins, J. G. (2005). *Hypnotherapeutic techniques*. New York: Brunner-Routledge.

Jensen, M. P., & Patterson, D. R. (2006). Hypnotic treatment of chronic pain. *Journal of Behavioral Medicine, 29*, 95–124.

McCarthy, P. (2001). Hypnosis in obstetrics and gynecology. In L. E. Fredericks (Ed.), *The use of hypnosis in surgery and anesthesiology* (pp. 163–211). Springfield, IL: Charles C. Thomas.

Olness, K., & Kohn, D. (1996). *Hypnosis and hypnotherapy with children* (3rd ed.). New York: Guilford.

Paterson, D. R. Clinical hypnosis in pain control and management (unpublished manuscript). Washington, DC: American Psychological Association.

Spiegel, H., & Spiegel, D. (2004). *Trance and treatment: Clinical uses of hypnosis*. Washington, DC: American Psychiatric Association Publishing.

Thomson, L. (2005). Hypnotic intervention therapy with surgical patients. *Hypnos, 32*(2), 88–96.

Watkins, J. G., & Barabasz, A. F. (2008). *Advanced hynotherapy: Hypnodynamic techniques*. New York: Routledge.

Yapko, M. (2005). *Sleeping soundly: Enhancing your ability to sleep well using hypnosis*. Fallbrook, CA: Yapko Publications.

References

Alladin, A. (2006). Cognitive hypnotherapy for treating depression. In R. A. Chapman (Ed.), *The clinical use of hypnosis in cognitive behavior therapy: A practitioner's casebook* (pp. 139–187). New York: Springer.

Alladin, A. (2007). *Handbook of cognitive hypnotherapy for depression: An evidence-based approach.* Philadelphia: Lippincott Williams & Wilkins.

Alladin, A., & Alibhai, A. (2007). Cognitive hypnotherapy for depression: An empirical investigation. *International Journal of Clinical and Experimental Hypnosis, 55*(2), 147–166.

American Psychiatric Association. (2000). *Diagnostic and statistical manual of mental disorders* (4th ed., text rev.). Washington, DC: Author.

Anderson, K., Barabasz, M., Barabasz, A., & Warner, D. (2000). Efficacy of Barabasz's instant alert hypnosis in the treatment of ADHD with neurotherapy. *Child Study Journal, 30*(1), 51–62.

Banks, S. M., & Kerns, R. D. (1996). Explaining high rates of depression in chronic pain: A diathesis-stress framework. *Psychological Bulletin, 119*, 95–110.

Barabasz, A. (1977). *New techniques in behavior therapy and hypnosis.* South Orange, NJ: Power Publishers.

Barabasz, A. (1982). Restricted environmental stimulation and the enhancement of hypnotizability: Pain, EEG alpha, skin conductance and temperature responses. *International Journal of Clinical and Experimental Hypnosis, 30*(2), 147–166.

Barabasz, A. (1984). Antarctic isolation and imaginative involvement-preliminary findings: A brief communication. *International Journal of Clinical and Experimental Hypnosis, 3*, 296–301.

Barabasz, A. (2000). EEG markers of alert hypnosis: The induction makes a difference. *Sleep and Hypnosis, 2*(4), 164–169.

Barabasz, A. (2001). The 2000 special issue on AD/HD, QEEG, neurotherapy and hypnosis: A review. *Journal of Neurotherapy, 4*(3), 99–101.

Barabasz, A. (2005–2006). Whither spontaneous hypnosis: A critical issue for practitioners and researchers. *American Journal of Clinical Hypnosis, 48*(2-3), 91–98.

Barabasz, A., & Barabasz, M. (1989). Effects of restricted environmental stimulation: Enhancement of hypnotizability for experimental and chronic pain control. *International Journal of Clinical and Experimental Hypnosis, 37,* 217–223.

Barabasz, A., & Barabasz, M. (2000). Treating AD/HD with hypnosis and neurotherapy. *Child Study Journal, 30*(1), 25–42.

Barabasz, A., & Barabasz, M. (2006). Effects of tailored and manualized hypnotic inductions for complicated irritable bowel syndrome patients. *International Journal of Clinical and Experimental Hypnosis, 54*(1), 100–112.

Barabasz, A., & Barabasz, M. (2008). Hypnosis and the brain. In M. Nash & A. Barnier (Eds.), *Contemporary hypnosis research.* New York: W. W. Norton & Company.

Barabasz, A., Barabasz, M., Jensen, S., Calvin, S., Trevisan, M., & Warner, D. (1999). Cortical event related potentials show the structure of hypnotic suggestions is crucial. *International Journal of Clinical and Experimental Hypnosis, 47*(1), 5–22.

Barabasz, A., & Christensen, C. (2006). Age regression: Tailored versus scripted inductions. *American Journal of Clinical Hypnosis, 48*(4), 251–261.

Barabasz, A., Higley, L., Christensen, C., & Barabasz, M. (in press). Hypnosis in the treatment of genital human papillomavirus in females. *International Journal of Clinical and Experimental Hypnosis.*

Barabasz, A., & Perez, N. (2007) Salient findings: Hypnotizability as a core construct and the clinical utility of hypnosis. *International Journal of Clinical and Experimental Hypnosis, 55*(3), 372–379.

Barabasz, A., & Watkins, J. G. (2005). *Hypnotherapeutic techniques.* New York: Brunner-Routledge.

Barabasz, M. (2007). Efficacy of hypnotherapy in the management of eating disorders. *International Journal of Clinical and Experimental Hypnosis, 55*(3), 330–347.

Barber, J. (1996). *Hypnosis and suggestion in the treatment of pain: A clinical guide.* New York: W. W. Norton & Company.

Barber, T. X. (1969). *Hypnosis: A scientific approach.* New York: Van Nostrand Reinhold.

Barber, T. X., & Glass, L. B. (1962). Significant factors in hypnotic behavior. *Journal of Abnormal and Social Psychology, 74,* 222–228.

Barlow, D. (2002). *Anxiety and its disorders: The nature and treatment of anxiety and panic* (2nd ed.). New York: Guilford Press.

Bauer, K., & McCanne, T. (1980). An hypnotic technique for treating insomnia. *International Journal of Clinical and Experimental Hypnosis, 28,* 1–5.

Becker, P. (1993). Chronic insomnia: Hypnotherapeutic intervention in six cases. *American Journal of Clinical Hypnosis, 36*(2), 98–105.

Benham, G., Woody, E. Z., Wilson, K. S., & Nash, M. R. (2006). Expect the unexpected: Ability, attitude, and responsiveness to hypnosis. *Journal of Personality and Social Psychology, 91,* 342–350.

Bennett, H. (1993). Preparing for surgery and medical procedures. In D. Goleman & J. Gurin (Eds.), *Mind-body medicine* (pp. 401–427). Yonkers, NY: Consumer Reports Books.

Blankfield, R. P. (1991). Suggestion, relaxation, and hypnosis as adjuncts in the care of surgery patients: A review of the literature. *American Journal of Clinical Hypnosis, 33,* 172–186.

Boothby, J. L., Thorn, B. E., Stroud, M. W., & Jensen, M. P. (1999). Coping with pain. In D. C. Turk & R. J. Gatchel (Eds.), *Psychosocial factors in pain* (pp. 343–359). New York: Guilford Press.

Borkovec, T., & Fowles, D. (1973). Controlled investigation of the effects of progressive and hypnotic relaxation on insomnia. *Journal of Abnormal Psychology, 82*(1), 153–158.

Bower, G. H., & Sivers, H. (1998). Cognitive impact of traumatic events. *Development and Psychopathology, 10*(4), 625–653.

Brown, C., Albrecht, R., Pettit, H., McFadden, T., & Schermer, C. (2000). Opioid and benzodiazepine withdrawal syndrome in adult burn patients. *America Journal of Surgery, 66,* 367–370.

Brown, D. P., & Fromm, E. (1990). Enhancing affective experience and its expression. In D. C. Hammond (Ed.), *Hypnotic suggestions and metaphors* (pp. 322–324). New York: W.W. Norton & Company.

Brown, D., & Hammond, C. (2007). Evidence-based clinical hypnosis for obstetrics, labor and delivery, and preterm labor. *International Journal of Clinical and Experimental Hypnosis, 55*(3), 282–299.

Burns, D. (1999). *Feeling good: The new mood therapy.* New York: Plume.

Bryant, R. A., Guthrie, R. M., Moulds, M. L., & Nixon, R. D. (2005). The additive benefit of hypnosis and cognitive-behavioral therapy in treating acute stress disorder. *Journal of Consulting and Clinical Psychology, 73,* 334–340.

Bryant, R. A., Guthrie, R. M., Moulds, M. L., Nixon, R. D., & Felmingham, K. (2003). Hypnotizability and posttraumatic stress disorder: A prospective study. *International Journal of Clinical & Experimental Hypnosis, 51*(4), 382–389.

Butler, L. D., Duran, R. E., Jasiukaitis, P., Koopman, C., & Spiegel, D. (1996). Hypnotizability and traumatic experience: A diathesis-stress model of dissociative symptomatology. *American Journal of Psychiatry, 153,* 42–63.

Butler, L. D., Symons, B. K., Henderson, S. L., Shortliffe, L. D., & Spiegel, D. (2005). Hypnosis reduces distress and duration of an invasive medical procedure for children. *Pediatrics, 115,* 77–85.

Cahill, L. (1997). The neurobiology of emotionally influenced memory: Implications for understanding traumatic memory. *Annals of the New York Academy of Sciences, 821*, 238–246.

Chambless, D. L., & Hollon, S. D. (1998). Defining empirically-supported therapies. *Journal of Consulting and Clinical Psychology, 66*, 7–18.

Cherny, N., Ripamonti, C., Pereira, J., Davis, C., Fallon, M., McQuay, H., et al. (2001). Strategies to manage the adverse effects of oral morphine: An evidence-based report. *Journal of Clinical Oncology, 19*, 2542–2554.

Christensen, C. (2005). Preferences for descriptors of hypnosis: A brief communication. *International Journal of Clinical and Experimental Hypnosis, 53*(3), 281–289.

Christensen, C., Barabasz, A., & Barabasz, M. (2009). Effects of an affect bridge for age regression. *International Journal of Clinical and Experimental Hypnosis, 57*, 4.

Cochran, H. (2003). Diagnose and treat primary insomnia. *Nurse Practitioner, 28*, 13–29.

Crum, R., Storr, C., Chan, Y.-F., & Ford, D. (2004). Sleep disturbance and risk for alcohol-related problems. *American Journal of Psychiatry, 161*, 1197–1203.

Cyna, A. M., Andrew, M. I., & McAuliffe, G. L. (2006). Hypnosis for pain relief in labour and childbirth: A systematic review. *British Journal of Anaesthesia, 93*, 505–511.

Daitch, C. (2007). *Affect regulation toolbox: Practical and effective hypnotic interventions for the over-reactive client.* New York: W. W. Norton & Company.

DeAngelis, T. (2008). Priming for the new role. *Monitor on Psychology, 39*(8), 29–31.

Edinger, J. D., Wohlgemuth, W. K., Krystal, A. D., & Rice, J. R. (2005). Behavioral insomnia therapy for fibromyalgia patients: A randomized clinical trial. *Archives of Internal Medicine, 28*, 2527–2535.

Elkins, G., Jensen, M., & Patterson, D. (2007). Hypnotherapy in the management of chronic pain. *International Journal of Clinical and Experimental Hypnosis, 55*(3) 251–263.

Emmerson, G. (2003). *Ego state therapy.* Williston, VT: Crown.

Erickson, M. H. (1967). *Advanced techniques of hypnosis and therapy.* New York: Grune & Stratton.

Erickson, M., & Rossi, E. (1979). *Hypnotherapy: An exploratory casebook.* New York: Irvington.

Esdaile, J. (1846). *Mesmerism in India and its practical application in surgery and medicine.* London: Longman, Brown, Green, and Longmans. (Reissued as *Hypnosis in medicine and surgery*, 1957, New York: Julian Press.)

Evans, S., Tsao, J. C. I., & Zeltzer, L. K. (2008). Complementary and alternative medicine for acute procedural pain in children. *Alternative Therapies, 14*, 52–56.

Everett, J. J., Patterson, D. R., & Chen, A. C. (1990). Cognitive and behavioral treatments for burn pain. *The Pain Clinic, 3*(3), 133–145.

Evidence-based practice in clinical hypnosis—Parts I and II [Special issue]. (2007). *International Journal of Clinical and Experimental Hypnosis, 55*(2-3).

Faymonville, M. E., Meurisse, M., & Fissette, J. (1999). Hypnosedation: A valuable alternative to traditional anaesthetic techniques. *Acta Chirurgica Belgica, 99*, 141–146.

Felt, B., Hall, H., Olness, K., Kohen, D. P., Berman, B. D., Broffman, G., et al. (1998). Wart regression in children: Comparison of relaxation-imagery to topical treatment and equal time interventions. *American Journal of Clinical Hypnosis, 41*, 130–137.

Fields, H. L. (2007). Should we be reluctant to prescribe opioids for chronic non-malignant pain? *Pain, 129*, 233–234.

Fingelkurts, A., Fingelkurts, A., Kallio, S., & Revonsuo, A. (2007). Cortex functional connectivity as a neurophysiological correlate of hypnosis: An EEG case study. *Neuropsychologia, 45*, 1452–1462.

Flammer, E., & Alladin, A. (2007). The efficacy of hypnotherapy in the treatment of psychosomatic disorders: Meta-analytical evidence. *International Journal of Clinical and Experimental Hypnosis, 55*(3), 348–371.

Flory, N., Martinez-Salazar, G., & Lang, E. (2007). Hypnosis for acute distress management during medical procedures. *International Journal of Clinical and Experimental Hypnosis, 55*(3), 315–329.

Ford, D., & Kamerow, D. (1989). Epidemiologic study of sleep disturbances and psychiatric disorders: An opportunity for prevention? *Journal of the American Medical Association, 262*, 1479–1484.

Fordyce, W. E. (1976). *Behavioral methods for chronic pain and illness.* St. Louis, MO: Mosby.

Frankel, F. H., & Orne, M. T. (1976). Hypnotizability and phobic behavior. *Archives of General Psychiatry, 33*(10), 1259–1271.

Frenay, M. C., Faymonville, M. E., Devlieger, S., Albert, A., & Vanderkelen, A. (2001). Psychological approaches during dressing changes of burned patients: A prospective randomised study comparing hypnosis against stress reducing strategy. *Burns, 27*(8), 793–799.

Frischholz, E. J., Blumstein, R., & Spiegel, D. (1982). Comparative efficacy of hypnotic behavioral training and sleep-trance hypnotic induction: Comment on Katz. *Journal of Consulting and Clinical Psychology, 50*, 777–779.

Frischholz, E. J., Spiegel, D., Trentalange, M. J., & Spiegel, H. (1987). The Hypnotic Induction Profile and absorption. *American Journal of Clinical Hypnosis, 30*(2), 87–93.

Fromm, E., & Kahn, S. (1990). *Self-hypnosis: The Chicago paradigm*. New York: Guildford Press.

Ginandes, C. S. (2003). Can medical hypnosis accelerate post-surgical wound healing? Results of a clinical trial. *American Journal of Clinical Hypnosis, 45*(4), 333–351.

Glaser, R., Kiecolt-Glaser, J. K., Marucha, P. T., MacCallum, R. C., Laskowski, B. F., & Malarkey, W. B. (1999). Stress related changes in proinflammatory cytokine production in wounds. *Archives of General Psychiatry, 56*, 450–456.

Golden, W. (2007). Cognitive-behavioral hypnotherapy in the treatment of irritable-bowel-syndrome-induced agoraphobia. *International Journal of Clinical and Experimental Hypnosis, 55*(2), 131–146.

Gotlib, I. H., & Goodman, S. H. (1999). Children of parents with depression. In W. K. Silverman & T. H. Ollendick (Eds.), *Developmental issues in the clinical treatment of children* (pp. 415–432). Boston: Allyn & Bacon.

Gotlib, I. H., & Hammen, C. L. (2002). Introduction. In I. H. Gotlib & C. L. Hammen (Eds.), *Handbook of depression* (pp. 1–20). New York: Guilford Press.

Graci, G., & Hardie, J. (2007). Evidence-based hypnotherapy for the management of sleep disorders. *International Journal of Clinical and Experimental Hypnosis, 55*(3), 300–314.

Gruzelier, J., Champion, A., Fox, P., Rollin, M., McCormack, S., Catalan, P., et al. (2002). Individual differences in personality, immunology and mood in patients undergoing self-hypnosis training for the successful treatment of a chronic viral illness, HSV-2. *Contemporary Hypnosis, 19*(4), 149–166.

Hammond, C. (2007). Review of the efficacy of clinical hypnosis with headaches and migraines. *International Journal of Clinical and Experimental Hypnosis, 55*(2), 207–219.

Harmon, T. M., Hynan, M. T., & Tyre, T. E. (1990). Improved obstetric outcomes using hypnotic analgesia and skill mastery combined with childbirth education. *Journal of Consulting and Clinical Psychology, 58*, 47–73.

Hewson-Bower, B. and Drummond, P. D. (1996). Secretory immunoglobulin A increases during relaxation in children with and without recurrent upper respiratory tract infections. *J Dev Behav Pediatr, 17*: 311–316.

Hewson-Bower, B. and Drummond, P. D. (2001). Psychological treatment for recurrent symptoms of colds and flu in children. *J Psychosom Research, 51*: 369–377.

Hilgard, E. R. (1965). *Hypnotic susceptibility*. New York: Harcourt, Brace & World.

Hilgard, E. R. (1979). *A saga of hypnosis: Two decades of the Stanford Laboratory of Hypnosis Research 1957–1979*. Unpublished manuscript, Stanford University, California.

Hilgard, E. R., & Hilgard, J. R. (1975). *Hypnosis in the relief of pain.* Los Altos, CA: William Kauffman.

Hilgard, E. R., & Tart, C. (1966). Responsiveness to suggestions following waking and imagination instructions and following induction of hypnosis. *Journal of Abnormal Psychology, 71*(3), 196–208.

Horowitz, M. (1986) *Stress response syndromes* (2nd ed.). Northvale, NJ: Nathan Aronson.

Hull, C. (2002). *Hypnosis and suggestibility: An experimental approach.* Bancyfelin, Carmarthen, Wales: Crown House. (Original work published 1933.)

Integration of behavioral and relaxation approaches into the treatment of chronic pain and insomnia. NIH Technology Assessment Panel on Integration of Behavioral and Relaxation Approaches into the Treatment of Chronic Pain and Insomnia. (1996). *Journal of the American Medical Association, 276,* 313–318.

Irritable bowel syndrome [Special issue]. (2006). *International Journal of Clinical and Experimental Hypnosis, 54*(1).

Jensen, M. P., Barber, J., Hanley, M. A., Engel, J. M. Romano, J. M., Cardenas, D. D., et al. (2008). Long-term outcome of hypnotic analgesia treatment for chronic pain in persons with disabilities. International Journal of Clinical and Experimental Hypnosis, 56, 156–169.

Jensen, M. P., Hanley, M. A., Engel, J. M., Romano, J. M., Barber, J., Cardenas, D. D., et al. (2005). Hypnotic analgesia for chronic pain in persons with disabilities: A case series. *International Journal of Clinical and Experimental Hypnosis, 53,* 198–228.

Jensen, M. P., McArthur K. D., Barber, J., Hanley, M. A., Engel, J. M., Romano, J. M., et al. (2006). Satisfaction with, and the beneficial side effects of, hypnotic analgesia. *International Journal of Clinical and Experimental Hypnosis, 54,* 432–447.

Jensen, M. P., & Patterson, D. R. (2006). Hypnotic treatment of chronic pain. *Journal of Behavioral Medicine, 29,* 95–124.

Jensen, M. P., & Patterson, D. R. (2008). Hypnosis in the relief of pain and pain disorders. In A. Barnier & M. R. Nash (Eds.), Contemporary hypnosis research (2nd ed.) (pp. 503–533). Oxford, UK: Oxford University Press.

Just, N., & Alloy, L. (1997). The response styles theory of depression: Tests and an extension of the theory. *Journal of Abnormal Psychology, 106,* 221–229.

Kahn, S., & Fromm, E. (Eds.). (2001). *Changes in the therapist.* Mahwah, NJ: Lawrence Erlbaum Associates.

Kessler, R. C., McGongale, K. A., Zhao, S., Nelson, C. B., Hughes, M., Eshleman, S., et al. (1994). Lifetime and 12-month prevalence of DSM-III-R psychiatric disorders in the United States: Results from the National Comorbidity Survey. *Archives of General Psychiatry, 51,* 8–19.

Kessler, R. C., Sonnega, A., Bromet, E., Hughes, M., & Nelson, C. B. (1995). Posttraumatic stress disorder in the National Comorbidity Survey. *Archives of General Psychiatry, 52*(12), 1048–1060.

Kiecolt-Glaser, J. K., Marucha, P. T., Atkinson, C., & Glaser, R. (2001). Hypnosis as a modulator of cellular immune dysregulation during acute stress. *Journal of Consulting & Clinical Psychology, 6994*, 674–682.

Killeen, P., & Nash, M. (2003). The four causes of hypnosis. *International Journal of Clinical and Experimental Hypnosis, 51*(3), 195–231.

Kirsch, I. (1996). Hypnotic enhancement of cognitive-behavioral weight loss treatments: Another meta-reanalysis. *Journal of Consulting and Clinical Psychology, 64*, 517–519.

Kirsch, I., Montgomery, G., & Sapirstein, G. (1995). Hypnosis as an adjunct to cognitive-behavioral psychotherapy: A meta-analysis. *Journal of Consulting and Clinical Psychology, 63*, 214–220.

Kluft, R. P. (1986). Clinical corner. *International Society for the Study of Multiple Personality and Dissociation Newsletter, 4*, 4–5.

Kluft, R. P. (1992). The use of hypnosis with dissociative disorders. *Psychiatric Medicine, 10*(4), 31–46.

Koe, G. (1989). Hypnotic treatment of sleep terror disorder: A case report. *American Journal of Clinical Hypnosis, 32*(1), 36–40.

Kohen, D. P., & Zajac, R. (2007). Self-hypnosis training for headaches in children and adolescents. *Journal of Pediatrics, 150*, 635–639.

Kosslyn, S., Thompson, W., Constantine-Ferrando, M., Alpert, N., & Spiegel, D. (2000). Hypnotic visual illusion alters color processing in the brain. *American Journal of Psychiatry, 157*, 1279–1284.

Kuttner, L. (1986). *No fears, no tears: Children with cancer coping with pain.* Vancouver, Canada: Canadian Cancer Society.

Kuttner, L. (1999). *No fears, no tears: 13 years later.* Vancouver, Canada: Canadian Cancer Society.

Lang, E. V., Benotsch, E. G., Fick, L. J., Lutgendorf, S., Berbaum, K. S., Logan, H., et al. (2000). Adjunctive nonpharmacologic analgesia for invasive medical procedures: A randomized trial. *Lancet, 355*, 1486–1490.

Lang, E. V., Berbaum, K., Faintuch, S., Hatsiopoulou, O., Halsey, N., Li, X., et al. (2006). Adjunctive self-hypnotic relaxation for outpatient medical procedures: A prospective randomized trial with women undergoing large core breast biopsy. *Pain, 126*, 155–164.

Lang, E. V., Berbaum, K. S., Pauker, S. G., Faintuch, S., Salazar, G. M., Lutgendor, S., et al. (2008). Beneficial effects of hypnosis and adverse effects of empathic attention during percutaneous tumor treatment: When being nice does not suffice. *Journal of Vascular and Interventional Radiology, 19*, 897–905.

Lang, E. V., Hatsiopoulou, O., Koch, T., Berbaum, K., Lutgendorf, S., Kettenmann, E., et al. (2005). Can words hurt? Patient-provider interactions during invasive medical procedures. *Pain, 114*, 303–309.

Lang, E. V., Joyce, J. S., Spiegel, D., Hamilton, D., & Lee, K. K. (1996). Self-hypnotic relaxation during interventional radiological procedures: Effects on pain perception and intravenous drug use. *International Journal of Clinical & Experimental Hypnosis, 44*(2), 106–119.

Lang, E. V., Lutgendorf, S., Logan, H., Benotsch, E., Laser, E., & Spiegel, D. (1999). Nonpharmacologic analgesia and anxiolysis for interventional radiological procedures. *Seminars Interventional Radiology, 16*, 113–123.

Lang, E. V., & Rosen, M. (2002). Cost analysis of adjunct hypnosis for sedation during outpatient interventional procedures. *Radiology, 222*, 375–382.

Letts, P. J., Baker, P. R. A., Ruderman, J., & Kennedy, K. (1993). The use of hypnosis in labor and delivery: A preliminary study. *Journal of Women's Health, 2*, 335–341.

Levin, P., Lazrove, S., & van der Kolk, B. (1999). What psychological testing and neuroimaging tell us about the treatment of posttraumatic stress disorder by eye movement desensitization and reprocessing. *Journal of Anxiety Disorder, 13*, 1–2, 159–172.

Littner, M., Hirshkowitz, M., Kramer, M., Kapen, S., Anderson, W., Bailey, D., et al. (2003). Practice parameters for using polysomnography to evaluate insomnia: An update. *Sleep, 26*(6), 754–757.

Lu, D. P., & Lu, G. P. (1996). Hypnosis and pharmacological sedation for medically compromised patients. *Compendium of Continuing Education in Dentistry, 17*(1), 32, 34–36, 38–40.

Lynn, S., & Cardena, E. (2007). Hypnosis and the treatment of posttraumatic conditions: An evidence-based approach. *International Journal of Clinical and Experimental Hypnosis, 55*, 167–188.

Lynn, S., & Kirsch, I. (2006). *Essentials of clinical hypnosis: An evidence-based approach*. Washington, DC: American Psychological Association.

Lynn, S. J., Kirsch, I., Barabasz, A., Cardena, E., & Patterson, D. (2000). Hypnosis as an empirically supported intervention: The state of the evidence and a look to the future. *International Journal of Clinical and Experimental Hypnosis, 48*, 2, 239–259.

Marc, I., Rainville, J., Masse, B., Verreault, R., Villancourt, L., Vallee, E., et al. (2008). Hypnotic analgesia intervention during first trimester pregnancy termination: An open randomized trial. *American Journal of Obstetrics and Gynecology, 199*, 469.e1–469.e9.

McCarthy, P. (1998). Hypnosis in obstetrics. *Australian Journal of Clinical and Experimental Hypnosis, 26*, 35–42.

McCarthy, P. (2001) Hypnosis in obstetrics and gynecology. In L. E. Fredericks (Ed.), *The use of hypnosis in surgery and anesthesiology* (pp. 163–211). Springfield, IL: Charles Thomas.

McConkey, K., Wende, V., & Barnier, A. J. (1999). Measuring change in the subjective experience of hypnosis. *International Journal of Clinical and Experimental Hypnosis, 47*, 23–39.

McGlashan, T. H., Evans, F. J., & Orne, M. T. (1969). The nature of hypnotic analgesia and placebo response to experimental pain. *Psychosomatic Medicine, 31*(3), 227–246.

Mehl-Madrona, L. (2004). Hypnosis to facilitate uncomplicated birth. *American Journal of Clinical Hypnosis, 46*, 299–312.

Melzack, R. (1990). The tragedy of needless pain. *Scientific American, 262*(2), 27–33.

Milstein, S. (2007, June). *Eye movements*. Paper presented at the EMDR Phase II workshop, Portland, OR.

Montgomery, G. H., Bovbjerg, D. H., Schnur, J. B., David, D., Goldfarb, A., & Weltz, C. R. (2007). A randomized clinical trial of a brief hypnosis intervention to control side effects in breast surgery patients. *Journal of the National Cancer Institute, 99*, 1304–1312.

Montgomery, G. H., David, D., Winkel, G., Silverstein, J. H., & Bovbjerg D. H. (2002). The effectiveness of adjunctive hypnosis with surgical patients: A meta-analysis. *Anesthesia & Analgesia, 94*(6), 1639–1645.

Montgomery, G. H., DuHamel, K. N., & Redd, W. H. (2000). A meta-analysis of hypnotically induced analgesia: How effective is hypnosis? *International Journal of Clinical and Experimental Hypnosis, 48*, 138–153.

Moore, J. D., & Bona, J. R. (2001). Depression and dysthymia. *Medical Clinics of North America, 85*(3), 631–644.

Morgan, A. H., & Hilgard, E. R. (1979). The Stanford Hypnotic Clinical Scale for Children. *American Journal of Clinical Hypnosis, 21*, 148–169.

Morgan, A., & Hilgard, J. (1975). The Stanford Hypnotic Clinical Scale for Adults. In E. Hilgard & J. Hilgard (Eds.), *Hypnosis in the relief of pain* (pp. 134–147). Los Altos, CA: Kaufmann.

Morgan, A. H., Johnson, D. L., & Hilgard, E. R. (1974). The stability of hypnotic susceptibility: A longitudinal study. *International Journal of Clinical & Experimental Hypnosis, 22*, 249–257.

Mott, T., Jr. (1982). The role of hypnosis in psychotherapy. *American Journal of Clinical Hypnosis, 24*(4), 241–248.

Murray, C. J. L., & Lopez, A. D. (Eds.). (1996). *The global burden of disease: A comprehensive assessment of mortality and disability from diseases, injuries, and risk factors in 1990 and projected to 2020*. Cambridge, MA: Harvard University Press.

Nash, M. (2005). The importance of being earnest when crafting definitions: Science and Scientism are not the same thing. *International Journal of Clinical and Experimental Hypnosis, 53*, 265–280.

Neron, S., & Stephenson, R. (2007). Effectiveness of hypnotherapy with cancer patients' trajectory: Emesis, acute pain, analgesia, and anxiolysis in procedures. *International Journal of Clinical and Experimental Hypnosis, 55*(3), 264–282.

Nijenhuis, E. R., Spinhoven, P., van Dyck R., van der Hart O., & Vanderlinden, J. (1998). Degree of somatoform and psychological dissociation in dissociative disorder is correlated with reported trauma. *Journal of Trauma and Stress, 11*, 711–730.

Nolen-Hoeksema, S. (1991). Responses to depression and their effects on the duration of depressive episodes. *Journal of Abnormal Psychology, 100*, 569–582.

Olness, K., & Kohen, D. P. (1996). *Hypnosis and hypnotherapy with children* (3rd ed.). New York: Guilford Press.

Olness, K., MacDonald, J., & Uden, D. (1987). A prospective study comparing self hypnosis, propranolol and placebo in management of juvenile migraine. *Pediatrics, 79*, 593–597.

O'Neill, L. M., Barnier, A. J., & McConkey, K. (1999). Treating anxiety with self-hypnosis and relaxation. *Contemporary Hypnosis, 16*(2), 68–80.

Orne, M. T. (1959). The nature of hypnosis: Artifact and essence. *Journal of Abnormal and Social Psychology, 48*, 277–299.

Orne, M. T., Hilgard, E. R., Spiegel, H., Spiegel, D., Crawford, H. J., Evans, F. J., et al. (1979). The relation between the Hypnotic Induction Profile and the Stanford Hypnotic Susceptibility Scales, Forms A and C. *International Journal of Clinical and Experimental Hypnosis, 27*, 85–102.

Oster, M. I. (1994). Psychological preparation for labor and delivery using hypnosis. *American Journal of Clinical Hypnosis, 37*, 12–21.

Oster, M. I. (2000). Contemporary methods in hypnotic preparation for childbirth. *CRNA: The Clinical Forum for Nurse Anesthetists, 11*, 160–166.

Overlade, D. C. (1986). First aid for depression. In E. T. Dowd & J. M. Healy (Eds.), *Case studies in hypnotherapy* (pp. 23–33). New York: Guilford Press.

Patterson, D. R. (1996). Burn pain. In J. Barber (Ed.), *Hypnosis and suggestion in the treatment of pain* (pp. 267–302). New York: W.W. Norton & Company.

Patterson, D. R., Everett, J. J., Burns, G. L., & Marvin, J. A. (1992). Hypnosis for the treatment of burn pain. *Journal of Consulting and Clinical Psychology, 5*, 713–717.

Patterson, D. R., & Jensen, M. P. (2003). Hypnosis and clinical pain. *Psychological Bulletin, 29*, 495–521.

Patterson, D. R., & Ptacek, J. T. (1997). Baseline pain as a moderator of hypnotic analgesia for burn injury treatment. *Journal of Consulting and Clinical Psychology, 65,* 60–67.

Patterson, D. R., & Sharar, S. (1997). Treating pain from severe burn injuries. *Advances in Medical Psychotherapy, 9,* 55–71.

Patterson, D. R., & Sharar, S. (2001). Burn pain. In J. Loeser (Ed.), *Bonica's management of pain* (3rd ed., pp. 780–787). Philadelphia: Lippincott Williams & Wilkins.

Patterson, D. R., Tininenko, J., & Ptacek, J. T. (2006). Pain during burn hospitalization predicts long-term outcome. *Journal of Burn Care and Research, 27*(5), 719–726.

Paulson, S. (2007, June). *Integrating EMDR and ego state therapy.* Paper presented at the EMDR Phase II workshop, Portland, OR.

Paykel, E. S., & Priest, R. G. (1992). Recognition and management of depression in general practice: Consensus statement. *British Medical Journal, 305,* 1198–1202.

Perry, C., & Mullen, G. (1975). The effects of hypnotic susceptibility on reducing smoking behavior treated by an hypnotic technique. *Journal of Clinical Psychology, 31*(3), 498–505.

Piccione, C., Hilgard, E. R., & Zimbardo, P. G. (1989). On the degree of stability of measured hypnotizability over a 25-year period. *Journal of Personality and Social Psychology, 57*(2), 289–295.

Pincus, H. A., & Pettit, A. R. (2001). The societal costs of chronic major depression. *Journal of Clinical Psychiatry, 62*(Suppl. 6), 5–9.

Rainville, P., & Price, D. (2003). Hypnosis phenomenology and neurobiology of consciousness. *International Journal of Clinical and Experimental Hypnosis, 51*(2), 105–129.

Romano, J. M., & Turner, J. A. (1985). Chronic pain and depression: Does the evidence support a relationship? *Psychological Bulletin, 97,* 18–34.

Sánchez-Armáss, O., Barabasz, A., & Barabasz, M. (2007). Estandarizacion De La Escala Stanford De Susceptibilidad Hipnotica, Forma C, En Una Muesstra Mexicana. *Ensenanza E Investigacion En Psicologia, 12*(1), 131–146.

Sapp, M. (1991). Hypnotherapy and test anxiety: Two cognitive-behavioral constructs. The effects of hypnosis in reducing test anxiety and improving academic achievement in college students. *Australian Journal of Clinical Hypnotherapy and Hypnosis, 12*(1), 26–41.

Sapp, M. (1992). Relaxation and hypnosis in reducing anxiety and stress. *Australian Journal of Clinical Hypnotherapy & Hypnosis, 13*(2), 39–55.

Sarbin, T. R., & Coe, W. C. (1972). *Hypnosis: A social-psychological analysis of influence communication.* New York: Holt, Rinehart & Winston.

Satcher, D. (2000). Mental health: A report of the Surgeon General—Executive summary. *Professional Psychology: Research and Practice*, *31*(1), 5–13.

Scharff, L., Marcus, D., & Masek, B. (2002). A controlled study of minimal-contact thermal biofeedback treatment in children with migraine. *Journal of Pediatric Psychology*, *27*(2), 109–119.

Schoenberger, N. E. (1996). Cognitive-behavioral hypnotherapy for phobic anxiety. In S. J. Lynn, I. Kirsch, & J. W. Rhue (Eds.), *Casebook of clinical hypnosis* (pp. 33–49). Washington, DC: American Psychological Association.

Schoenberger, N. E. (2000). Research on hypnosis as an adjunct to cognitive-behavioral psychotherapy. *International Journal of Clinical and Experimental Hypnosis*, *48*, 154–169.

Schoenberger, N. E., Kirsch, I., Gearan, P., Montgomery, G. M., & Pastyrnak, S. L. (1997). Hypnotic enhancement of a cognitive behavioral treatment for public speaking anxiety. *Behavior Therapy*, *28*, 127–140.

Schwartz, G. (1984). Psychophysiology of imagery and healing: A systems perspective. In A. A. Sheikh (Ed.), *Imagination and healing* (pp. 35–50). Amityville, NY: Baywood.

Schwartz, G., Fair, P. L., Salt, P., Mandel, M. R., & Klerman, G. L. (1976). Facial muscle patterning in affective imagery in depressed and nondepressed subjects. *Science*, *192*, 489–491.

Shapiro, F. (2002). EMDR 12 years after its introduction: Past and future research. *Journal of Clinical Psychology*, *58*(1), 1–22.

Silver, S., Rogers, S., Knipe, J., & Colelli, G. (2005). EMDR therapy following the 9/11 terrorist attacks: A community-based intervention project in New York City. *International Journal of Stress Management*, *12*(1), 29–42.

Smith, J. T., Barabasz, A., & Barabasz, M. (1996). A comparison of hypnosis and distraction in severely ill children undergoing painful medical procedures. *Journal of Counseling Psychology*, *43*(2), 187–195.

Spasojevic, J., & Alloy, L. (2001). Rumination as a common mechanism relating depressive risk factors to depression. *Emotion*, *1*, 25–37.

Spiegel, D. (1989). Hypnosis in the treatment of victims of sexual abuse. *Psychiatric Clinics of North America*, *12*, 295–305.

Spiegel, D. (1992). The use of hypnosis in the treatment of PTSD. *Psychiatric Medicine*, *10*(4), 21–30.

Spiegel, D. (1997). Trauma, dissociation, and memory. *Annals of New York*, *821*, 225–237.

Spiegel, D. (1998). Hypnosis and implicit memory: Automatic processing of explicit content. *American Journal of Clinical Hypnosis*, *40*(3), 231–240.

Spiegel, D. (2007). *Finding Flow in the Brain*. Workshop presented at the American Society for Clinical Hypnosis (ASCH)–Society for Clinical and Experimental Hypnosis (SCEH) Joint Annual Scientific Meeting, Dallas TX, January 19–23.

Spiegel, D., Hunt, T., & Dondershine, H. E. (1988). Dissociation and hypnotizability in posttraumatic stress disorder. *American Journal of Psychiatry, 145*(3), 301–305.

Spiegel, D., & Vermetten, E. (2007). Post-traumatic stress disorder: Medicine or politics (not both). *Lancet, 369,* 992.

Spiegel, H. (1972). An eye-roll test for hypnotizability. *American Journal of Clinical Hypnosis, 15,* 25–28.

Spiegel, H. (1974). The grade 5 syndrome: The highly hypnotizable person. *International Journal of Clinical & Experimental Hypnosis, 22*(4), 303–319.

Spiegel, H., & Spiegel, D. (1978). *Trance and treatment: Clinical uses of hypnosis*. Washington, DC: American Psychiatric Press.

Spiegel, H., & Spiegel, D. (2004). *Trance and treatment: Clinical uses of hypnosis* (2nd ed.). Arlington, VA: American Psychiatric Publishing.

Stanton, H. E. (1989). Hypnotic relaxation and the reduction of sleep onset insomnia. *International Journal of Psychosomatics, 36,* 64–68.

Stanton, H. E. (1990). Dumping the "rubbish." In C. D. Hammond (Ed.), *Handbook of hypnotic suggestions and metaphors* (p. 313). New York: W. W. Norton & Company.

Stanton, H. E. (1994). Self-hypnosis: One path to reduced test anxiety. *Contemporary Hypnosis, 11*(1), 14–18.

Starfrace, S. (1994). Hypnosis in the treatment of panic disorder with agoraphobia. *Australian Journal of Clinical and Experimental Hypnosis, 22,* 73–76.

Stern, D. B., Spiegel, H., & Nee, J. C. (1978). The Hypnotic Induction Profile: Normative observations, reliability and validity. *American Journal of Clinical Hypnosis, 21*(2-3), 109–133.

Tellegen, A., & Atkinson, G. (1974). Openness to absorbing and self-altering experiences ("absorption"), a trait related to hypnotic susceptibility. *Journal of Abnormal Psychology, 83*(3), 268–277.

Thase, M. (2000). Treatment issues related to sleep and depression. *Journal of Clinical Psychiatry, 61*(Suppl. 11), 46–50.

Thompson, S. C. (1981). Will it hurt less if I can control it? A complex answer to a simple question. *Psychological Bulletin, 90,* 89–100.

Thomson, L. (2005). Hypnotic intervention therapy with surgical patients. *Hypnos, 32*(2), 88–96.

Turk, D. C. (2002). A cognitive-behavioral perspective on treatment of chronic pain patients. In D. C. Turk & R. J. Gatchel (Eds.), *Psychological approaches to pain management: A practitioner's handbook* (pp. 138–158). New York: Guilford Press.

van der Kolk, B. A. (1994). The body keeps the score: Memory and the evolving psychobiology of posttraumatic stress. *Harvard Review of Psychiatry, 1*(5), 253–265.

van der Kolk, B. A. (2007, January). *New frontiers in trauma treatment.* Paper presented in Seattle, Washington.

van der Kolk, B. A., McFarlane, A., & Alexander, C. (Eds.). (1996). *Traumatic stress: The effects of overwhelming experience on mind, body, and society.* New York: Guildford.

van der Kolk, B. A., Pelcovitz, D., Roth, S., Mandel, F. S., McFarlane, A., & Herman, J. L. (1996). Dissociation, somatization, and affect dysregulation: The complexity of adaptation of trauma. *American Journal of Psychiatry, 153*(7), 83–93.

Vermetten, E., & Bremner, D. J. (2004). Functional brain imaging and the induction of traumatic recall: A cross-correlational review between neuroimaging and hypnosis. *International Journal of Clinical Experimental Hypnosis, 52,* 280–312.

Vermetten, E., Dorahy, M., & Spiegel, D. (Eds.). (2007). *Traumatic dissociation: Neurobiology and treatment.* Washington, DC: American Psychiatric Press.

Vermetten, E., & Spiegel, D. (2007). Perceptual processing and traumatic stress: Contributions from hypnosis. In E. Vermetten, M. Dorahy, & D. Spiegel (Eds.), *Traumatic dissociation: Neurobiology and treatment* (pp. 239–259). Washington, DC: American Psychiatric Press.

Vlaeyen, J. W., de Jong, J., Geilen, M., Heuts, P. H., & van Breukelen, G. (2002). The treatment of fear of movement/(re)injury in chronic low back pain: Further evidence on the effectiveness of exposure in vivo. *Clinical Journal of Pain, 18,* 251–261.

Vlaeyen, J. W., & Linton, S. J. (2000). Fear-avoidance and its consequences in chronic musculoskeletal pain: A state of the art. *Pain, 85,* 317–332.

Wade, T. J., & Cairney, J. (2000). Major depressive disorder and marital transition among mothers: Results from a national panel study. *Journal of Nervous and Mental Disease, 188,* 741–750.

Wain, H. J. (2004). Reflections on hypnotizability and its impact on successful surgical hypnosis: A sole anesthetic for septoplasty. *American Journal of Clinical & Hypnosis, 46,* 313–321.

Warner, D. A., Barabasz, A., & Barabasz, M. (2000). The efficacy of Barabasz's alert hypnosis and neurotherapy on attentiveness, impulsivity and hyperactivity in children with ADHD. *Child Study Journal, 30*(1), 43–49.

Watkins, J. G., & Barabasz, A. (2008). *Hypnoanalytic techniques* (2nd ed.). New York: Brunner-Routledge.

Watkins, J. G., & Watkins, H. (1997). *Ego states: Theory and therapy.* New York: W. W. Norton & Company.

Weathers, F. W., Ruscio, A. M., & Keane, T. M. (1999). Psychometric properties of nine scoring rules for the Clinician-Administered Posttraumatic Stress Disorder Scale. *Psychological Assessment, 11,* 124–133.

Weitzenhoffer, A. M. (1980). Hypnotic susceptibility revisited. *American Journal of Clinical Hypnosis, 22*(3), 130–147.

Weitzenhoffer, A., & Hilgard, E. (1962). *Stanford Hypnotic Susceptibility Scale: Form C.* Palo Alto, CA: Consulting Psychologists Press.

Whitehouse, W. G., Dinges, D. F., Orne, E. C., Keller, S. E., Bates, B. L., Bauer, N. K., et al. (1996). Psychosocial and immune effects of self-hypnosis training for stress management throughout the first semester of medical school. *Psychosomatic Medicine, 58,* 249–263.

World Health Organization. (1998). *Well-being measures in primary healthcare/The Depcare Project.* Copenhagen: WHO Regional Office for Europe.

World Health Organization. (2001). *World Health Report 2001: Mental health: New understanding, new hope.* Geneva: Author.

Yapko, M. (1992). *Hypnosis and the treatment of depressions: Strategies for change.* New York: Brunner-Mazel.

Yapko, M. (2003). *Trancework: An introduction to the practice of clinical hypnosis* (3rd ed.). New York: Brunner-Routledge.

Yapko, M. (2005). *Sleeping soundly: Enhancing your ability to sleep well using hypnosis.* Fallbrook, CA: Yapko Publications.

Yapko, M. (Ed.). (2006). *Hypnosis and treating depression: Applications in clinical practice.* New York: Routledge.

Youngren, M. A., & Lewinshon, P. M. (1980). The functional relation between depression and problematic interpersonal behavior. *Journal of Abnormal Psychology, 89,* 333–341.

Zeltzer, L., & LeBaron, S. (1982). Hypnosis and nonhypnotic techniques for reduction of pain and anxiety during painful procedures in children and adolescents with cancer. *The Journal of Pediatrics, 101,* 1032–1035.

Index